Programming Interview Problems: Dynamic Programming

Leonardo Rossi

Programming Interview Problems: Dynamic Programming (with solutions in Python)

Contents

Preface

Over the last decade, many companies have adopted the FANG-style interview process for software engineer positions: programming questions that involve an algorithm design step, and often require competitive programming solving techniques.

The advantages and disadvantages of this style of interview questions are highly debated, and outside the scope of this book. What is important is that the questions that are asked pose serious challenges to candidates, thus require thorough preparation.

The class of problems that are by far the most challenging is *dynamic programming*. This is due to a combination of dynamic programming being rarely used in day-to-day work, and the difficulty of finding a solution in a short amount of time, when not having prior experience with this method.

This book presents 25 dynamic programming problems that are most commonly encountered in interviews, and several of their variants. For each problem, multiple solutions are given, including a gradual walkthrough that shows how one may reach the answer. The goal is not to memorize solutions, but to understand how they work and learn the fundamental techniques, such that new, previously unseen problems can be solved with ease.

The solutions are very detailed, showing example walkthroughs, verbal explanations of the solutions, and many diagrams and drawings. These were designed in a way that helps both verbal and visual learners grasp the material with ease. The code implementation usually comes last, accompanied by unit tests and complexity/performance analysis.

A particular focus has been put on code clarity and readability: during the interview, we are expected to write code as we would on the job. This means that the code must be tidy, with well-named variables, short functions that do one thing, modularity, comments describing why we do certain things etc. This is, sadly, unlike most other material on dynamic programming that one may find online, in competitive programming resources, or even in well-known algorithm design textbooks. In fact, the poor state of the material on this topic is the main reason I wrote this book.

I hope that you find this book useful for preparing to get the job you wish for. Whether you like the book or not, I would appreciate your feedback through a book review.

Good luck with your interviews!

General advice for the interview

Find out in advance what kind of questions will be asked. Usually, they are in one or more of the following categories: coding, algorithm design (with or without implementation), domain-specific questions, theoretical questions, behavioral questions, live coding, debugging, one-day assignments or pair programming. You should know what you need to prepare for.

For programming questions, do not jump directly to writing code, even if the solution looks obvious. First, ask clarification questions and go over some simple examples, to make sure you understand the requirements well. Then, you may sketch a solution and discuss it with the interviewer. Several iterations might be needed in case of correctness or performance issues. Only once they agree that the solution looks fine, proceed with implementing it.

Treat the interview questions not like problems, but real job assignments. Take them seriously and solve them thoroughly, like a professional.

Treat your interviewers as colleagues, with whom you must work together to solve the assignment. Shift into the mindset that you are already on the same team. Discuss and interact with them the same way you would with colleagues on the job.

Write tidy, clean code—as much as possible given the time you have. Try to follow typical coding style guidelines for your language. For Python, you can find good guidelines at www.python.org/dev/peps/pep-0008 and google.github.io/styleguide/pyguide.html.

Do not forget to ask about the size of the data your code needs to handle—this is important to determine the time complexity of your solution.

If you cannot find the fastest algorithm needed to solve the problem, propose a slower one. Sometimes you might get an idea (or a hint from the interviewer) to make it faster once you write it. But even if you do not, any solution is better than no solution.

Try to be quick in your answer. Interviewers usually plan to ask follow-up questions. If you do not have sufficient time left for these, your result may be poor, even if you answered the original question well.

1   The Fibonacci sequence

Return the n-th number in the Fibonacci sequence. The first two numbers in the Fibonacci sequence are equal to 1; any other number is equal to the sum of the preceding two numbers.

Example: for n = 6, the first 6 numbers of the sequence are [1, 1, 2, 3, 5, 8] so the result is 8.

Solution 1: brute force, $O(2^n)$ time

A straightforward solution is to implement the function recursively:

```python
def fibonacci(n):
    if n <= 2:
        return 1
    return fibonacci(n - 1) + fibonacci(n - 2)
```

The above code is correct but too slow due to redundancies. We can see this if we add logging to the function:

```python
import inspect
def stack_depth():
    return len(inspect.getouterframes(inspect.currentframe())) - 1


def fibonacci(n):
    print("{indent}fibonacci({n}) called".format(
                indent="  " * stack_depth(), n=n))
    if n <= 2:
        return 1
    return fibonacci(n - 1) + fibonacci(n - 2)


fibonacci(6)
```

We changed the code to print the argument passed to the fibonacci function. The message is indented by the call stack depth, so that we can see better which function call is causing which subsequent calls. Running the above code prints:

```
fibonacci(6) called
  fibonacci(5) called
    fibonacci(4) called
      fibonacci(3) called
        fibonacci(2) called
        fibonacci(1) called
      fibonacci(2) called
    fibonacci(3) called
      fibonacci(2) called
      fibonacci(1) called
    fibonacci(4) called
```

```
fibonacci(3) called
  fibonacci(2) called
  fibonacci(1) called
fibonacci(2) called
```

That's a lot of calls! If we draw the call graph, we can see that it's an almost full binary tree:

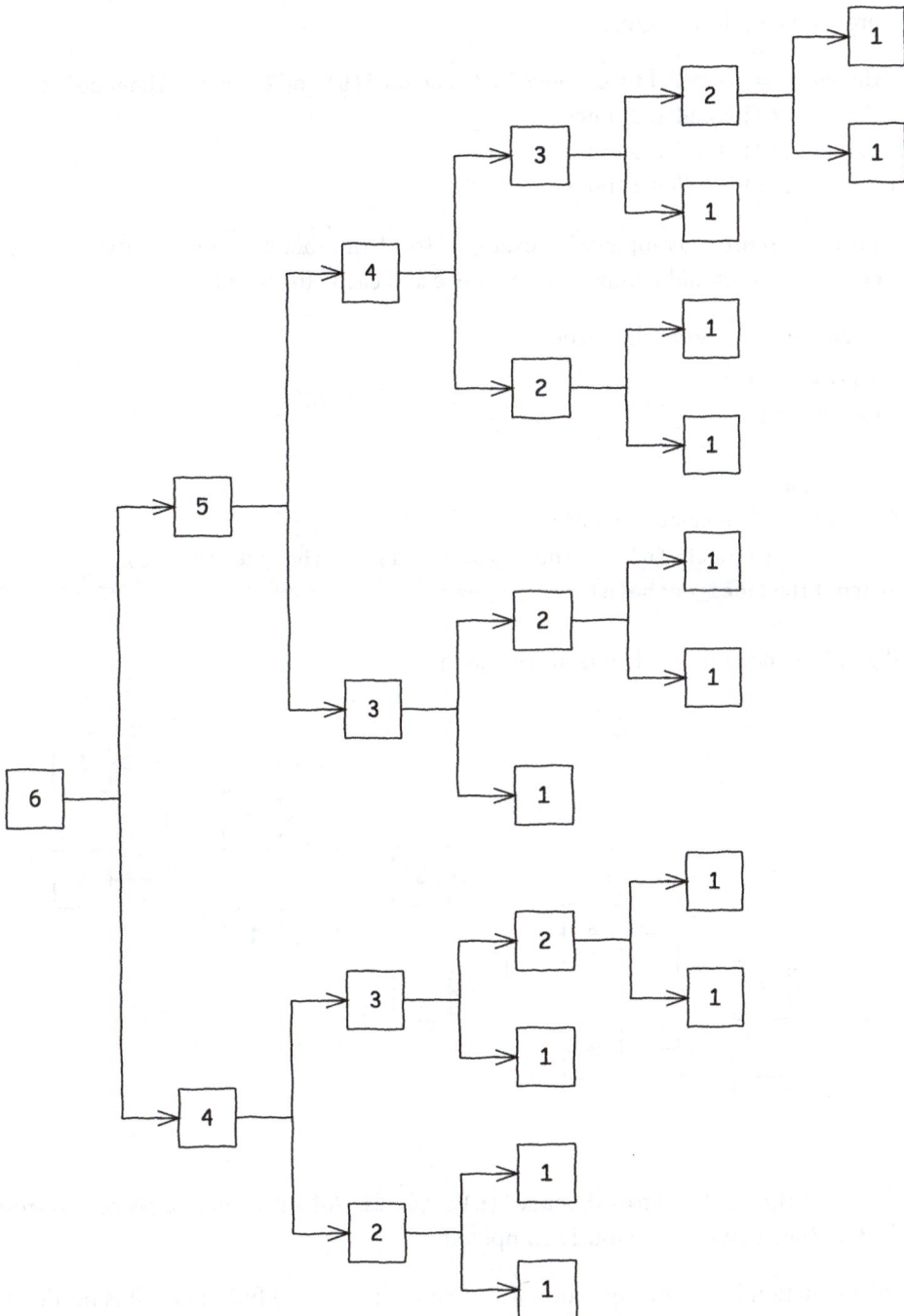

Notice that the height of the binary tree is n (in this case, 6). The tree is almost full, thus it has $O(2^n)$ nodes. Since each node represents a call of our function, our algorithm has exponential complexity.

Solution 2: dynamic programming, top-down

We can optimize the previous solution by avoiding redundant computations. These redundancies are visible in the call graph:

- `fibonacci(4)` is called twice, once by `fibonacci(5)` and once by `fibonacci(6)`;
- `fibonacci(3)` is called 3 times;
- `fibonacci(2)` is called 5 times;
- `fibonacci(1)` is called 3 times.

It does not make sense to compute, for example, the 4-th Fibonacci number twice, since it does not change. We should compute it only once and cache the result.

Let's use a dictionary to store the cache:

```python
fibonacci_cache = {}
def fibonacci(n):
    if n <= 2:
        return 1
    if n not in fibonacci_cache:
        fibonacci_cache[n] = fibonacci(n - 1) + fibonacci(n - 2)
    return fibonacci_cache[n]
```

The call graph of the optimized code looks like this:

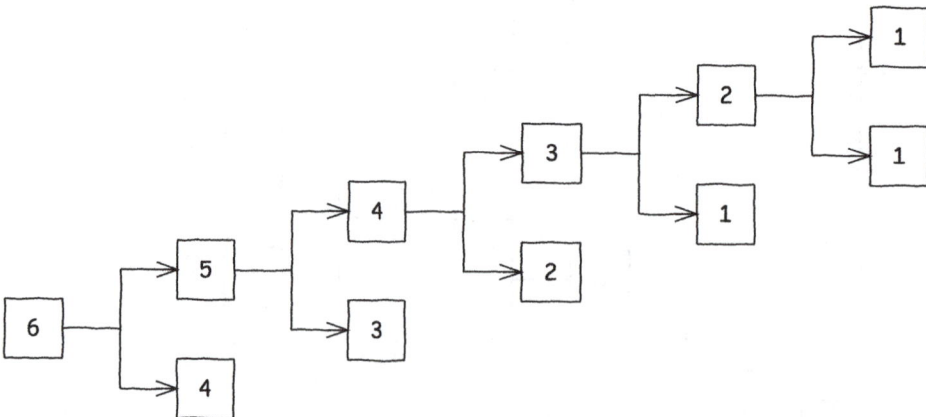

Notice how only the first call to `fibonacci(n)` recurses. All subsequent calls return from the cache the value that was previously computed.

This implementation has $O(n)$ time complexity, since exactly one function call is needed to compute each number in the series.

This strategy of caching the results of subproblems is called *dynamic programming*.

While the above code is correct, there are some code style issues:

- We introduced the global variable `fibonacci_cache`; it would be great if we could avoid global variables, since they impact code readability;
- The code is more complicated than before due to the cache manipulations.

We can avoid adding the global variable by using instead an attribute called `cache` that is attached to the function:

```python
def fibonacci(n):
    if n <= 2:
        return 1
    if not hasattr(fibonacci, 'cache'):
        fibonacci.cache = {}
    if n not in fibonacci.cache:
        fibonacci.cache[n] = fibonacci(n - 1) + fibonacci(n - 2)
    return fibonacci.cache[n]
```

The advantage is that the cache variable is now owned by the function, so no external code is needed anymore to initialize it. The disadvantage is that the code has become even more complicated, thus harder to read and modify.

A better approach is to keep the original function simple, and wrap it with a decorator that performs the caching:

```python
def cached(f):
    cache = {}
    def worker(*args):
        if args not in cache:
            cache[args] = f(*args)
        return cache[args]
    return worker


@cached
def fibonacci(n):
    if n <= 2:
        return 1
    return fibonacci(n - 1) + fibonacci(n - 2)
```

The good news is that Python 3 has built-in support for caching decorators, so there is no need to roll your own:

```python
from functools import lru_cache


@lru_cache(maxsize=None)
def fibonacci(n):
    if n <= 2:
```

```
        return 1
    return fibonacci(n - 1) + fibonacci(n - 2)
```

By default `lru_cache` is limited to 128 entries, with least-recently used entries evicted when the size limit is hit. Passing `maxsize=None` to `lru_cache` ensures that there is no memory limit and all values are cached. In practice, it might be preferable to set a limit instead of letting memory usage increase without bounds.

> **Prefer standard library functionality to rolling your own**
>
> Using the standard `lru_cache` decorator makes the code easier to read, since it has well-known behavior. The advantage over using a custom caching method is that the reader does not need to spend time to understand its details.

Solution 2: dynamic programming, bottom-up

While computing the Fibonacci sequence recursively is useful for pedagogical reasons, it is more intuitive to compute it iteratively starting from the smaller numbers, just like a human would do:

```
def fibonacci(n):
    series = [1, 1]
    while len(series) < n:
        series.append(series[-1] + series[-2])
    return series[-1]
```

The code has $O(n)$ time complexity, as well as $O(n)$ space complexity. In practice the performance is better than the recursive implementation, since there is no overhead due to extra function calls.

The space complexity can be reduced to $O(1)$ if we notice that we do not need to store the entire sequence, just the last two numbers:

```
def fibonacci(n):
    previous = 1
    current = 1
    for i in range(n - 2):
        next = current + previous
        previous, current = current, next
    return current
```

We have written an algorithm that starts from the smallest subproblem (the first two numbers in the sequence), then expands the solution to reach the original problem (the n-th number in the sequence). This approach is called *bottom-up* dynamic programming. By contrast, the previous approach of solving the problem recursively starting from the top is called *top-down* dynamic programming. Both approaches are equally valid; one or the other may be more intuitive, depending on the problem.

In the rest of the book, we will look at how we can apply dynamic programming to solving non-trivial problems. In general, we will show both top-down and bottom-up solutions. We will see that the top-down approach is often easier to understand and implement, however it offers less optimization opportunities compared to bottom-up.

2   Optimal stock market strategy

When evaluating stock market trading strategies, it is useful to determine the maximum possible profit that can be made by trading a certain stock. Write an algorithm that, given the daily price of a stock, computes the maximum profit that can be made by buying and selling that stock. Assume that you are allowed to own no more than 1 share at any time, and that you have an unlimited budget.

Example 1: The stock price over several days is [2, 5, 1]. The best strategy is to buy a share on the first day for price 2, then sell it on the second day for price 5, obtaining a profit of 3.

Example 2: The stock price over several days is [2, 5, 1, 3]. The best strategy is to buy a share on the first day for price 2, then sell it on the second day for price 5, obtaining a profit of 3; then buy it again on the third day for price 1, and sell it on the fourth day for price 3, obtaining an overall profit of 5.

Solution 1: dynamic programming, top-down, $O(n)$ time

The first idea that comes to mind while approaching this problem is using a state machine. This is because on any day, our state can be described by:

- whether we own the share or not;
- the amount of money we have.

Between the states of consecutive days, we have only four possible transitions:

- If at the end of the previous day we did not own the share:
  - buying the stock, so we now own it, but we have less money;
  - avoiding the stock, so we keep our money unchanged;
- If at the end of the previous day we owned the share:
  - selling the stock, so we no longer own it, and have more money;
  - holding the stock, so we keep both the stock and our money unchanged.

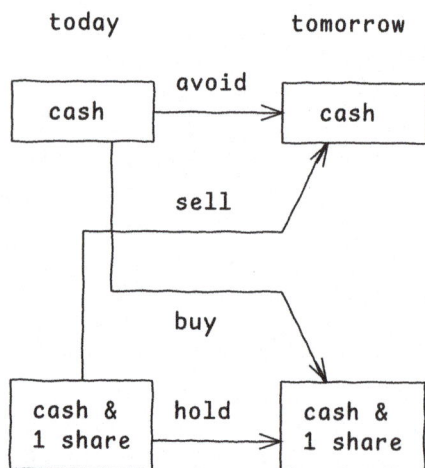

Knowing this, we can model the entire problem using a state machine. In our initial state, we have some amount of cash and no shares. In the final state, we have some other amount of cash (ideally higher), and no shares. In between, we have state transitions:

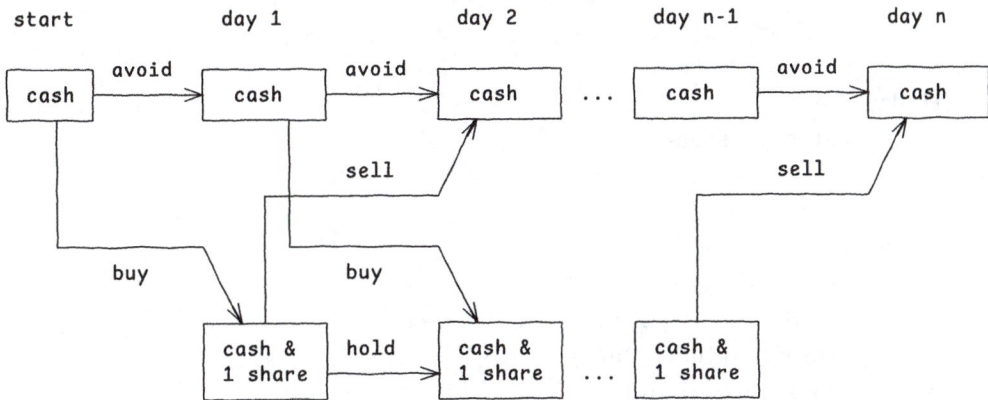

Solving the original problem can be reduced to finding a chain of transitions through this state machine, that yields the maximum profit.

Notice how our state during any day only depends on the state from the previous day. This is excellent: we can express our problem using a simple recurrence relation, just as we did for the Fibonacci sequence problem.

The structure of the solution using a recursive algorithm looks like this:

```python
def max_profit(daily_price):
    def get_best_profit(day, have_stock):
        """

        Returns the best profit that can be obtained by the end of the day.
        At the end of the day:
        * if have_stock is True, the trader must own the stock;
        * if have_stock is False, the trader must not own the stock.
        """

        # TODO ...
    # Final state: end of last day, no shares owned.
    last_day = len(daily_price) - 1
    no_stock = False
    return get_best_profit(last_day, no_stock)
```

Note that we defined a helper function `get_best_profit` which takes as parameters the identifiers of a state: the day number and whether we own the stock or not at the end of the day. We use `get_best_profit` to compute the profit for a specific state in the state machine.

Let's now implement the helper using a recurrence relation. We need to consider the previous states that can transition into the current state, and choose the best one:

```python
@lru_cache(maxsize=None)
def get_best_profit(day, have_stock):
    """
```

```
    Returns the best profit that can be obtained by the end of the day.
    At the end of the day:
    * if have_stock is True, the trader must own the stock;
    * if have_stock is False, the trader must not own the stock.
    """
    if day < 0:
        if not have_stock:
            # Initial state: no stock and no profit.
            return 0
        else:
            # We are not allowed to have initial stock.
            # Add a very large penalty to eliminate this option.
            return -float('inf')
    price = daily_price[day]
    if have_stock:
        # We can reach this state by buying or holding.
        strategy_buy = get_best_profit(day - 1, False) - price
        strategy_hold = get_best_profit(day - 1, True)
        return max(strategy_buy, strategy_hold)
    else:
        # We can reach this state by selling or avoiding.
        strategy_sell = get_best_profit(day - 1, True) + price
        strategy_avoid = get_best_profit(day - 1, False)
        return max(strategy_sell, strategy_avoid)
```

The first part of the helper implements the termination condition, i.e. handling the initial state, while the second part implements the recurrence. To simplify the logic of the recurrence we allow selling on any day including the first, but we ensure that selling on the first day would yield a negative profit, so it's an option that cannot be chosen as optimal.

> **Handle the termination condition early**
>
> It is preferable to handle the termination condition of a recursive function in a single place, as opposed to wrapping each call of the function with a check like if day < 0 . . . . Handling it early simplifies greatly the logic and makes the code easier to read.

Both the time and space complexity of this solution are $O(n)$. Note that it is important to cache the results of the helper function, otherwise the time complexity becomes exponential instead of linear.

Solution 2: dynamic programming, bottom-up, $O(n)$ time

Once we have implemented the top-down solution, it is easy to rewrite it as bottom-up: we start from the initial state, and iterate day by day until we reach the final state:

```python
def max_profit(daily_price):
    # Initial state: start from a reference cash amount.
    # It can be any value.
    # We use 0 and allow our cash to go below 0 if we need to buy a share.
    cash_not_owning_share = 0
    # High penalty for owning a stock initially:
    # ensures this option is never chosen.
    cash_owning_share = -float('inf')
    for price in daily_price:
        # Transitions to the current day, owning the stock:
        strategy_buy = cash_not_owning_share - price
        strategy_hold = cash_owning_share
        # Transitions to the current day, not owning the stock:
        strategy_sell = cash_owning_share + price
        strategy_avoid = cash_not_owning_share
        # Compute the new states.
        cash_owning_share = max(strategy_buy, strategy_hold)
        cash_not_owning_share = max(strategy_sell, strategy_avoid)
    # The profit is the final cash amount, since we start from
    # a reference of 0.
    return cash_not_owning_share
```

At each step, we only need to store the profit corresponding to the two states of that day. This is due to the state machine not having any transitions between non-consecutive days: we could say that at any time, the state machine does not "remember" anything from the days before yesterday.

The time complexity is $O(n)$, but the space complexity has been reduced to $O(1)$, since we only need to store the result for the previous day.

> **Bottom-up solutions often have smaller space complexity than top-down**
>
> It is very common (with some exceptions) that bottom-up solutions have lower memory requirements than top-down. This is due to the ability to control precisely what data we store and what data we discard: instead of a LRU cache policy, we can keep only the data we need. In addition, they do not suffer from the overhead of storing stack frames due to recursion, which is a hidden cost of the top-down solutions.

Variation: limited investment budget

In a variation of the problem, the investment budget is limited: we start with a fixed amount of money, and we are not allowed to buy a share if we cannot afford it (we cannot borrow money).

We can adjust the solution for this constraint:

```
def max_profit(daily_price, budget):
    # Initial state.
    cash_not_owning_share = budget
    # High penalty for owning a stock initially:
    # ensures this option is never chosen.
    cash_owning_share = -float('inf')
    for price in daily_price:
        # Transitions to the current day, owning the stock:
        strategy_buy = cash_not_owning_share - price
        strategy_hold = cash_owning_share
        # Transitions to the current day, not owning the stock:
        strategy_sell = cash_owning_share + price
        strategy_avoid = cash_not_owning_share
        # Compute the new states.
        cash_owning_share = max(strategy_buy, strategy_hold)
        if cash_owning_share < 0:
            # We cannot afford to buy the share at this time.
            # Add a high penalty to ensure we never choose this option.
            cash_owning_share = -float('inf')
        cash_not_owning_share = max(strategy_sell, strategy_avoid)
    return cash_not_owning_share - budget
```

Any time the optimal cash amount in a given state goes below zero, we replace it with negative infinity. This ensures that this path through the state machine will not be chosen. We only have to do this for the states where we own stock. In the states where we do not own stock, our cash amount never decreases from the previous day, so this check is not needed.

> **Expect follow-up questions**
>
> One of the most common mistakes candidates make is to assume that they have to solve a single problem during a time slot of the interview. Taking too long to solve it does not leave any time for follow-up questions, which puts the candidate at a disadvantage compared to others. An old Italian proverb applies here: *perfect is the enemy of good*. Do not get lost in too many details trying to make your solution perfect; reach an agreement with your interviewer on when it is good enough, so that you have time to take 1-2 follow-up questions such as this one.

Variation: limited number of transactions

In another variation of the problem, the total number of transactions that can be performed is bounded: the stock can only be sold up to a certain number of times tx_limit.

In this variation, the state machine needs to be adjusted so that it keeps track of multiple pieces of information:

- whether we own the stock or not at the end of the day;

- how many times we have sold the stock so far.

Instead of having only 2 states each day (for owning or not owning the stock), we now have up to 2 * tx_limit depending on how many times we have sold, per day. For each of these states, we have to compute the best amount of money we can earn.

The transitions between the states need to take into account the operation (buying, holding, selling, avoiding) and whether it leads to the next day state with the same transaction count or one higher.

We can write the following implementation:

```python
def max_profit(daily_price, tx_limit):
    # cash_not_owning_share[k] = amount of cash at the end of the day,
    # if we do not own the share, and we have sold k times so far.
    # Initially we have sold 0 times and we start from a reference
    # budget of 0. Any other state is invalid.
    cash_not_owning_share = [-float('inf')] * (tx_limit + 1)
    cash_not_owning_share[0] = 0
    # cash_owning_share[k] = amount of cash at the end of the day,
    # if we own the share, and we have sold k times so far.
    # Initially we do not own any stock, so set the state to invalid.
    cash_owning_share = [-float('inf')] * (tx_limit + 1)
    for price in daily_price:
        # Initialize the next day's states with -Infinity,
        # then update them with the best possible transition.
        cash_not_owning_share_next = [-float('inf')] * (tx_limit + 1)
        cash_owning_share_next = [-float('inf')] * (tx_limit + 1)
        for prev_tx_count in range(tx_limit):
            # Transition to the current day, owning the stock:
            strategy_buy = cash_not_owning_share[prev_tx_count] - price
            strategy_hold = cash_owning_share[prev_tx_count]
            # Transitions to the current day, not owning the stock:
            strategy_sell = cash_owning_share[prev_tx_count] + price
            strategy_avoid = cash_not_owning_share[prev_tx_count]
            # Compute the new states.
            if prev_tx_count < tx_limit:
                # Selling increases the tx_count by 1.
                cash_not_owning_share_next[prev_tx_count + 1] = max(
                        cash_not_owning_share_next[prev_tx_count + 1],
                        strategy_sell)
            # All other transitions keep tx_count the same.
            cash_not_owning_share_next[prev_tx_count] = max(
                    cash_not_owning_share_next[prev_tx_count],
                    strategy_avoid)
            cash_owning_share_next[prev_tx_count] = max(
                    cash_owning_share_next[prev_tx_count],
```

```
                        strategy_buy,
                        strategy_hold)
        cash_not_owning_share = cash_not_owning_share_next
        cash_owning_share = cash_owning_share_next
    # We have multiple final states, depending on how many times we sold.
    # The transaction limit may not have been reached.
    # Choose the most profitable final state.
    return max(cash_not_owning_share)
```

Master state machines

While you are reading this book, take your time to understand well how to model problems using state machines. Almost all dynamic programming problems can be solved this way. This skill is useful not just for interviews, but also in general in your software engineer career.

3   Change-making

Given a money amount and a list of coin denominations, provide the combination of coins adding up to that amount, that uses the fewest coins.

Example 1: Pay amount 9 using coin denominations [1, 2, 5]. The combination having the fewest coins is [5, 2, 2]. A suboptimal combination is [5, 1, 1, 1, 1]: it adds up to 9, but is using 5 coins instead of 3, thus it cannot be the solution.

Example 2: Pay amount 12 using coin denominations [1, 6, 10]. The combination having the fewest coins is [6, 6]. A suboptimal combination is [10, 1, 1].

Clarification questions

Q: What result should be returned for total amount 0?
A: The empty list [].

Q: Is it possible that the amount cannot be paid with the given coins?
A: Yes. For example, 5 cannot be paid with coins [2, 4]. In such a situation, return None.

Solution 1: dynamic programming, top-down, $O(nv)$ time

We can formulate a top-down dynamic programming solution if we model the problem as a recurrence. For any non-zero amount that has to be paid optimally using the given coins, we know that at least one of the coins has to be used. The problem is that we do not know which one. If we knew, we could use that as a starting point to reach a subproblem: we could subtract its value from the amount, then solve an instance of the problem for the remaining, smaller amount. We would continue in this way until the remaining amount becomes 0.

However, we do not know which coin to choose first optimally. In this situation, we have no other choice but try all possible options in brute-force style. For each coin, we subtract its value from the amount, then solve by recurrence the subproblem—this leads to a candidate solution for each choice of the first coin. Once we are done, we compare the candidate solutions and choose the one using the fewest coins.

Here is an example of how we would form the optimal change for amount 9, using coins [1, 2, 5]. We represent each amount as a node in a tree. Whenever we subtract a coin value from that amount, we add an edge to a new node with a smaller value. Please mind that the actual solution does not use trees, at least not explicitly: they are shown here only for clarity.

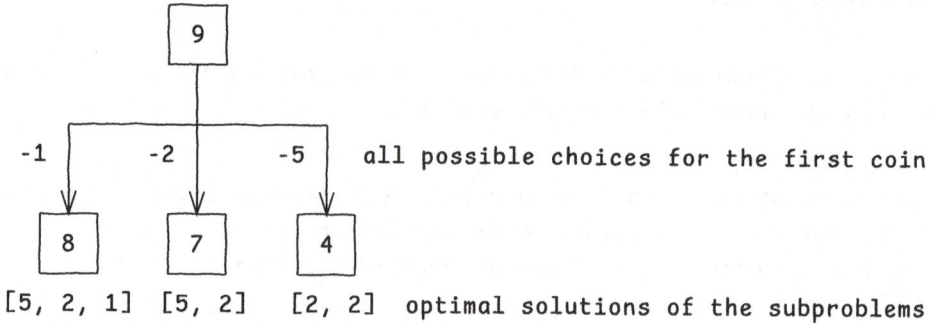

```
                    ┌───┐
                    │ 9 │
                    └─┬─┘
                      │
      ┌───────────────┼───────────────┐
     -1          -2 │              -5       all possible choices for the first coin
      │              │               │
      ▼              ▼               ▼
    ┌───┐          ┌───┐          ┌───┐
    │ 8 │          │ 7 │          │ 4 │
    └───┘          └───┘          └───┘
  [5, 2, 1]      [5, 2]        [2, 2]     optimal solutions of the subproblems
```

This diagram shows that for value 9, we have three options for choosing the first coin:

- We choose coin 1. We now have to solve the subproblem for value 9 − 1 = 8. Suppose its optimal result is [5, 2, 1]. Then we add coin 1 to create the candidate solution [5, 2, 1, 1] for 9.
- We choose coin 2. We now have to solve the subproblem for value 9 − 2 = 7. Suppose the optimal result is [5, 2]. We add to it coin 2 to create the candidate solution [5, 2, 2] for 9.
- We choose coin 5. We now have to solve the subproblem for value 9 − 5 = 4. The optimal result is [2, 2]. We add to it coin 5 to create the candidate solution [5, 2, 2] for 9.

Now that we are done solving the subproblems, we compare the candidate solutions and choose the one using the fewest coins: [5, 2, 2].

For solving the subproblems, we use the same procedure. The only difference is that we need to pay attention to two edge cases: the terminating condition (reaching amount 0), and avoiding choices where we are paying too much (reaching negative amounts). To understand these better, let's take a look at the subproblems:

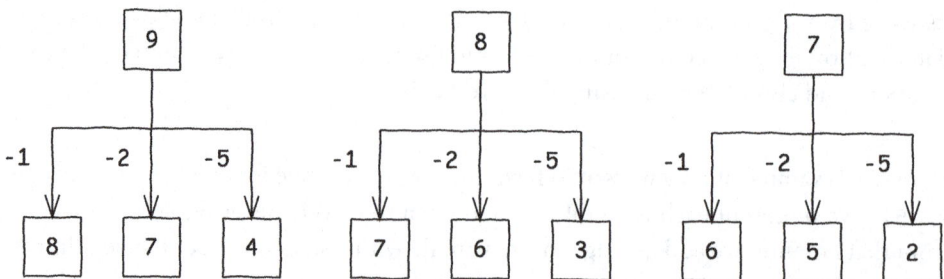

```
        [6]                      [5]                      [4]
   -1    -2    -5           -1    -2    -5           -1    -2    -5
  [5]   [4]   [1]          [4]   [3]   [0]          [3]   [2]   [x]

        [3]                      [2]                      [1]
   -1    -2    -5           -1    -2    -5           -1    -2    -5
  [2]   [1]   [x]          [1]   [0]   [x]          [0]   [x]   [x]
```

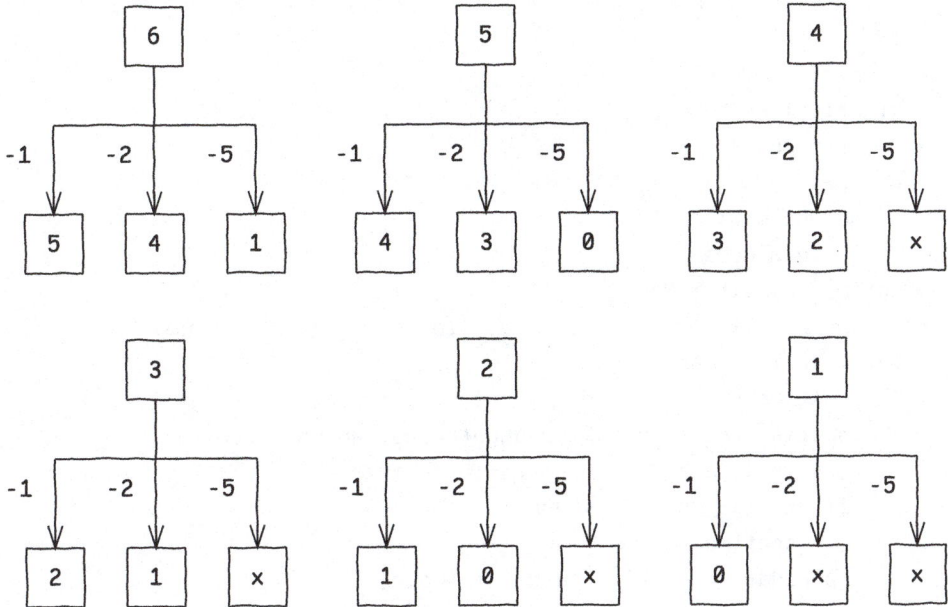

Drawing the subproblems helps us see clearly the edge cases:

- When the amount becomes 0, we have to stop the iteration, since the subproblem is solved and there is nothing left to be paid. We can see the 0 node in several of the subproblem trees.
- When the amount goes below zero, the given amount cannot be formed with that coin. For example, trying to pay amount 3 using coin 5 would require solving the subproblem for amount -2, which does not make sense.

In addition to that, we can also notice that there are many redundancies among the subproblems. This is very important, as it affects the performance of the algorithm. We originally thought about solving the problem using brute force, which results in a slow algorithm: $O(n^v)$, where n is the number of coins and v is the value of the amount we have to pay. In other words, the brute-force solution has exponential complexity, with very poor performance.

However, now that we know that there are redundancies among the subproblems, we can cache their results to reduce the complexity to only $O(nv)$: in each step we must try n coins, and we have up to v steps (in the worst case, we pay v with v coins of value 1). This result is great: we reduced the time complexity from exponential to polynomial!

We are now ready to write a first implementation of the recurrence, without caching (the brute-force, exponential complexity solution). This is because we want to focus on the logic of the recurrence, without distractions; we will add caching afterwards.

```python
def make_change(coins, amount):
    """
    Given a list of coin values, and an amount to be paid,
    returns the shortest list of coins that add up to that amount.
    If the amount to be paid is zero, the empty list is returned.
```

```python
        If the amount cannot be paid using the coins, None is returned.
        """
        # Handle payment of amount zero.
        if not amount:
            return []
        # Negative amounts cannot be paid.
        if amount < 0:
            return None
        optimal_result = None
        # Consider all the possible ways to choose the last coin.
        for coin in coins:
            # Solve a subproblem for the rest of the amount.
            partial_result = make_change(coins, amount - coin)
            # Skip this coin if the payment failed:
            if partial_result is None:
                continue
            candidate = partial_result + [coin]
            # Check if the candidate solution is better than the
            # optimal solution known so far, and update it if needed.
            if (optimal_result is None or
                    len(candidate) < len(optimal_result)):
                optimal_result = candidate
        return optimal_result
```

This algorithm implements the recurrence relation as explained above. Notice how we handle the edge cases at the beginning of the function, before making any recursive calls, to avoid infinite recursion and to keep the recursion logic as simple as possible.

> **Handle and eliminate edge cases early**
>
> Generally, it is preferrable to get edge cases out of the way as soon as possible, so that the rest of the implementation is kept simple. This improves substantially the readability of the code.

This implementation has exponential time complexity, since we have not implemented caching yet. Let's do that now.

Unfortunately, if we try to add caching simply adding the `lru_cache` decorator, we will have a nasty surprise:

```python
from functools import lru_cache


@lru_cache(maxsize=None)
def make_change(coins, amount):
    ...
```

This code throws the exception: `TypeError: unhashable type: 'list'`. This is caused by the inability to cache the argument `coins`. As a list, it is mutable, and the `lru_cache` decorator rejects it. The decorator supports caching only arguments with immutable types, such as numbers, strings or tuples. This is for a very good reason: to prevent bugs in case mutable arguments are changed later (in case of lists, via `append`, `del` or changing its elements), which would require invalidating the cache.

A joke circulating in software engineering circles says that there are only two hard problems in computer science: cache invalidation, naming things, and off-by-one errors. To address the former, the design of the `lru_cache` decorator takes the easy way out: it avoids having to implement cache invalidation at all by only allowing immutable arguments.

Still, we need to add caching one way or another. We can work around the `lru_cache` limitation if we notice that we do not actually need to cache the `coins` list—that is shared among all subproblems. We only need to pass the remaining amount to be paid. So we write a helper function that solves the subproblem, taking as argument only the amount. The coin list is shared between invocations.

One way to implement this is to make the helper function nested inside the `make_change` function, so that it has access to the `coins` argument of the outer function:

```python
def make_change(coins, amount):
    @lru_cache(maxsize=None)
    def helper(amount):
        ...
    return helper(amount)
```

Another way is to transform the `make_change` function into a method of a class, that stores the list of coins in a class member. The helper could then be written as another method of the class, ideally a private one. I think adding classes is overkill for what we have to do, so we will not discuss this approach.

Here is the full solution that uses nested functions:

```python
def make_change(coins, amount):
    """
    Given a list of coin values, and an amount to be paid,
    returns the shortest list of coins that add up to that amount.
    If the amount to be paid is zero, the empty list is returned.
    If the amount cannot be paid using the coins, None is returned.
    """

    @lru_cache(maxsize=None)
    def helper(amount):
        # Handle payment of amount zero.
        if not amount:
            return []
        # Negative amounts cannot be paid.
        if amount < 0:
            return None
```

```
        optimal_result = None
        # Consider all the possible ways to choose the last coin.
        for coin in coins:
            # Solve a subproblem for the rest of the amount.
            partial_result = helper(amount - coin)
            # Skip this coin if the payment failed:
            if partial_result is None:
                continue
            candidate = partial_result + [coin]
            # Check if the candidate solution is better than the
            # optimal solution known so far, and update it if needed.
            if (optimal_result is None or
                    len(candidate) < len(optimal_result)):
                optimal_result = candidate
        return optimal_result
    return helper(amount)
```

How many comments should we write?

Well-written comments improve code readability, however there is a trade-off: too many comments can be distracting, are a maintainability burden, and a sign that the code might not be clear enough. However, for interviews, I prefer leaning towards more verbosity, since we normally do not have time to refactor the code to perfection. Comments can compensate for that.

A good rule of thumb is to use comments to explain *why* the code is doing something. If you feel the need to explain *what* it is doing, it might be time to refactor that piece of code into an appropriately-named function. If you do not have time to refactor during the interview, you can add a comment like: "TODO: refactor into helper function."

Solution 2: dynamic programming, bottom-up, $O(nv)$ time

Once we have implemented the top-down solution, we can rewrite it as bottom-up: we start from the amount 0, and keep adding coins in all possible ways until reaching the amount to be paid:

```
def make_change(coins, amount):
    # solutions[k] = optimal list of coins that add up to k,
    #                or None if no solution is known for k
    solutions = [None] * (amount + 1)
    # Initial state: no coins needed to pay amount 0
    solutions[0] = []
    # Starting from amount 0, find ways to pay higher amounts
    # by adding coins.
    paid = 0
    while paid < amount:
```

```
        if solutions[paid] is not None:
            for coin in coins:
                next_paid = paid + coin
                if next_paid > amount:
                    continue
                if (solutions[next_paid] is None or
                    len(solutions[next_paid]) >
                    len(solutions[paid]) + 1):
                    solutions[next_paid] = solutions[paid] + [coin]
        paid += 1
    return solutions[amount]
```

This solution is iterative, which is an advantage compared to the top-down solution, since it avoids the overheads of recursive calls. However, for certain denominations, it wastes time by increasing the amount very slowly, in steps of 1 unit. For example, if `coins = [100, 200, 500]` (suppose we use bills), it does not make sense to advance in steps of 1.

In addition, a lot of space is wasted for amounts that cannot be paid. Let's see if we can come up with a better solution.

Solution 3: dynamic programming + BFS, bottom-up, $O(nv)$ time

We can optimize the bottom-up solution by using a queue of amounts to be handled, instead of an array. This helps in two ways: Firstly, it allows us to skip amounts that cannot be formed, thus reducing execution time. Secondly, by not having to store amounts that cannot be paid, memory usage is reduced.

Let's implement it:

```
def simplest_change(coins, amount):
    # solutions[k] = optimal list of coins that add up to amount k
    # Amounts that cannot be paid are not stored.
    solutions = {0: []}
    # List of amounts that can be paid but have not been handled yet.
    amounts_to_be_handled = collections.deque([0])
    # Iterate over amounts in breadth-first order.
    while amounts_to_be_handled:
        paid = amounts_to_be_handled.popleft()
        solution = solutions[paid]
        if paid == amount:
            # Due to BFS order, the first path reaching the
            # required amount is the one using the smallest number
            # of coins. Thus it is the optimal solution.
            return solution
        for coin in coins:
            next_paid = paid + coin
            if next_paid > amount:
```

```
            # We can safely ignore amounts overshooting the
            # target amount to be paid.
            continue
        if next_paid not in solutions:
            solutions[next_paid] = solution + [coin]
            amounts_to_be_handled.append(next_paid)
    # No combination of coins could match the required amount,
    # thus it cannot be paid.
    return None
```

Notice how we are treating the (sub)problem space as a graph, which is explored in breadth-first order (BFS). We start from the subproblem of forming the amount 0. From there, we keep expanding using all the possible coin choices until we reach the required amount.

Let's look at an example showing how the problem space exploration works for paying amount 9 with coins [1, 2, 5]. We start with amount 0 and explore by adding a coin in all possible ways. Here is the first level of the problem space graph:

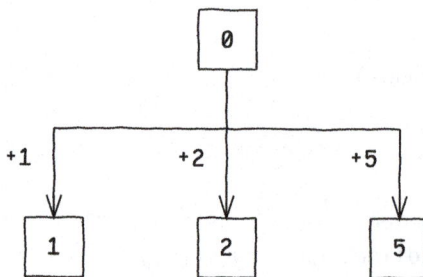

The first level contains all amounts that can be paid using a single coin. After this step, we have [1, 2, 5] in our BFS queue, which is exactly the list of nodes on the first level—hence the name of breadth-first search.

To fill in the second level of the problem space graph, we continue the exploration a step further for amounts 1, 2 and 5:

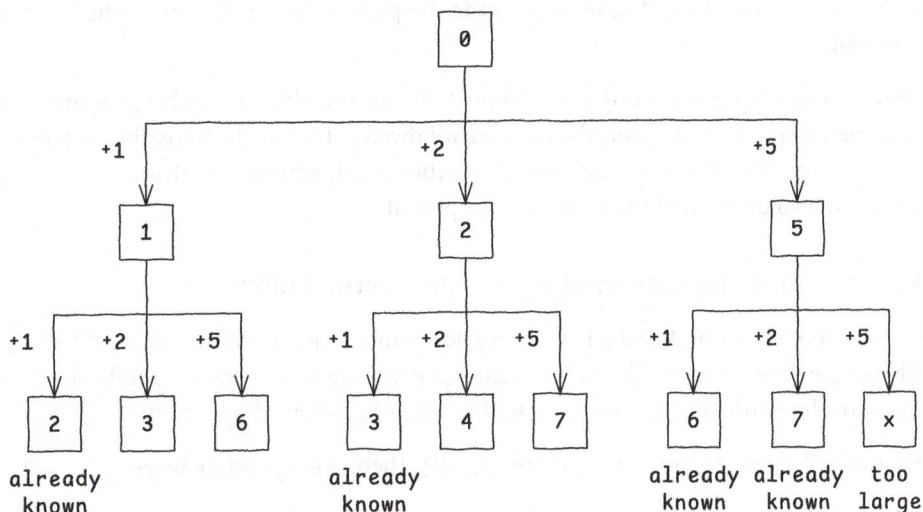

The second level contains all possible amounts that can be paid with 2 coins. After this step, we have [3, 6, 4, 7] in our BFS queue.

Notice that we discarded nodes corresponding to already known amounts, since these can be paid with a similar or better solution (fewer coins). We have also discarded amounts that exceed the value we have to pay (such as 10). This ensures that the graph size is bounded and that it contains only valid/optimal nodes.

We still have not found a way to pay our target amount, 9. Let's explore further, adding the third level of the problem space graph:

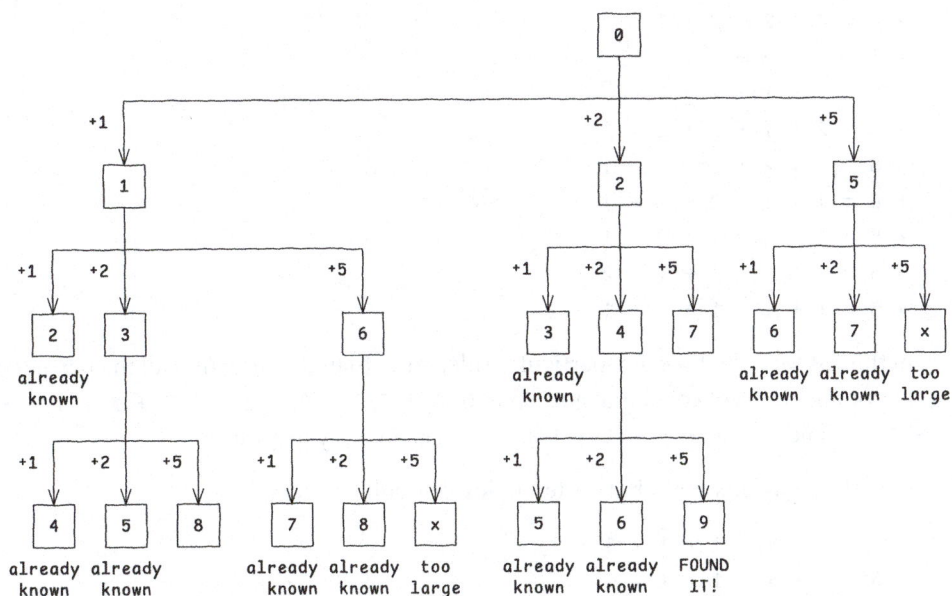

Note that as we reached the target amount 9, we stopped drawing the rest of the level. As it is on the third level of the tree, the amount can be paid with 3 coins. The combination is

2, 2 and 5, which can be found by walking the path from 0 to 9. This is the solution to the problem.

Note that the exploration order was important: the breadth-first order guarantees that each time we reach a new amount, the path we followed is the shortest possible in terms of number of coins used. Had we used instead another graph search algorithm, such as depth-first search, the solution might not have been optimal.

Variant: count the number of ways to pay (permutations)

Given a money amount and a list of coin denominations, count in how many ways it is possible to pay that amount. The order matters, i.e. paying with a coin of 1 followed by a coin of 2 is considered distinct from paying with a coin of 2 followed by a coin of 1.

Example: To pay amount 3 with coins [1, 2], there are 3 possible ways: 1 + 2, 2 + 1 and 1 + 1 + 1.

Solution: dynamic-programming, top-down, $O(nv)$

Let's analyze a slightly more complicated example: paying amount 6 with coins [1, 2, 5]. Here are all the possible ways to pay the amount:

- 6 = 5 + 1
- 6 = 1 + 5
- 6 = 2 + 2 + 2
- 6 = 2 + 2 + 1 + 1
- 6 = 2 + 1 + 2 + 1
- 6 = 2 + 1 + 1 + 2
- 6 = 1 + 2 + 2 + 1
- 6 = 1 + 2 + 1 + 2
- 6 = 1 + 1 + 2 + 2
- 6 = 2 + 1 + 1 + 1 + 1
- 6 = 1 + 2 + 1 + 1 + 1
- 6 = 1 + 1 + 2 + 1 + 1
- 6 = 1 + 1 + 1 + 2 + 1
- 6 = 1 + 1 + 1 + 1 + 2
- 6 = 1 + 1 + 1 + 1 + 1 + 1

From this list we do not see any particular rule, other than enumerating all the permutations of the combinations of coins that add up to 6 (1 + 5, 2 + 2 + 2, 2 + 2 + 1 + 1, 2 + 1 + 1 + 1 + 1 and 1 + 1 + 1 + 1 + 1 + 1). This is not very helpful.

Let's list the payments again but sorted in lexicographic order:

- 6 = 1 + 1 + 1 + 1 + 1 + 1
- 6 = 1 + 1 + 1 + 1 + 2
- 6 = 1 + 1 + 1 + 2 + 1
- 6 = 1 + 1 + 2 + 1 + 1
- 6 = 1 + 1 + 2 + 2

- 6 = 1 + 2 + 1 + 1 + 1
- 6 = 1 + 2 + 1 + 2
- 6 = 1 + 2 + 2 + 1
- 6 = 1 + 5
- 6 = 2 + 1 + 1 + 1 + 1
- 6 = 2 + 1 + 1 + 2
- 6 = 2 + 1 + 2 + 1
- 6 = 2 + 2 + 1 + 1
- 6 = 2 + 2 + 2
- 6 = 5 + 1

We can now see a pattern we can use to generate the list:

- Choose 1 as the first coin to pay and pay it. Then pay the rest of the amount (5) in all possible ways:
  - 5 = 1 + 1 + 1 + 1 + 1
  - 5 = 1 + 1 + 1 + 2
  - 5 = 1 + 1 + 2 + 1
  - 5 = 1 + 2 + 1 + 1
  - 5 = 1 + 2 + 2
  - 5 = 2 + 1 + 1 + 1
  - 5 = 2 + 1 + 2
  - 5 = 2 + 2 + 1
  - 5 = 5
- Then choose 2 as the first coin to pay and pay it. Then pay the rest of the amount (4) in all possible ways:
  - 4 = 1 + 1 + 1 + 1
  - 4 = 1 + 1 + 2
  - 4 = 1 + 2 + 1
  - 4 = 2 + 1 + 1
  - 4 = 2 + 2
- Finally, choose 5 as the first coin to pay and pay it. Then pay the rest of the amount (1) in all possible ways:
  - 1 = 1

We found a rule that reduces the problem to a smaller subproblem. The subproblems can be solved using the same pattern. Let's show the second iteration:

- Choose 1 as the first coin to pay and pay it. Then pay the rest of the amount (5) in all possible ways:
  - Choose 1 as the second coin to pay and pay it. Then pay the rest of the amount (4) in all possible ways:
    - 4 = 1 + 1 + 1 + 1
    - 4 = 1 + 1 + 2
    - 4 = 1 + 2 + 1
    - 4 = 2 + 1 + 1
    - 4 = 2 + 2

- Choose 2 as the second coin to pay and pay it. Then pay the rest of the amount (3) in all possible ways:
  - 3 = 1 + 1 + 1
  - 3 = 1 + 2
  - 3 = 2 + 1
- Choose 5 as the second coin to pay and pay it. There is nothing left to be paid.
- Then choose 2 as the first coin and pay it. Then pay the rest of the amount (4) in all possible ways:
  - Choose 1 as the second coin to pay and pay it. Then pay the rest of the amount (3) in all possible ways:
    - 3 = 1 + 1 + 1
    - 3 = 1 + 2
    - 3 = 2 + 1
  - Choose 2 as the second coin to pay and pay it. Then pay the rest of the amount (2) in all possible ways:
    - 2 = 1 + 1
    - 2 = 2
- Finally, choose 5 as the first coin and pay it. Then pay the rest of the amount (1) in all possible ways:
  - Choose 1 as the second coin to pay and pay it. There is nothing left to pay.

Notice that this method computes the number of ways to pay certain amounts, such as 4 or 3, several times. We have to cache the results to avoid exponential complexity due to the redundancies.

Now that we found a recursive rule, we can implement a top-down dynamic programming solution as follows:

```python
def count_ways_to_pay(coins, amount):
    @lru_cache
    def count_ways_helper(amount):
        # Nothing more left to pay: a single way.
        if amount == 0:
            return 1
        # Invalid payment: we paid too much so the amount that
        # remains is negative.
        if amount < 0:
            return 0
        num_ways = 0
        # Consider all the possible ways to choose the first coin:
        for first in coins:
            # Count the ways to pay the rest of the amount.
            num_ways += count_ways_helper(amount - first)
        return num_ways
    return helper(amount)
```

The time complexity is $O(nv)$, where n is the number of coins and v is the amount we have to pay.

Variant: count the number of ways to pay (combinations)

Given a money amount and a list of coin denominations, count in how many ways it is possible to pay that amount. The order does not matter, i.e. paying with a coin of 1 followed by a coin of 2 is considered the same as paying with a coin of 2 followed by a coin of 1, so it should be only counted once.

Example: To pay amount 3 with coins [1, 2], there are 2 possible ways: 1 + 2 and 1 + 1 + 1.

> **Counting combinations vs. permutations**
>
> Please pay attention and take your time to understand the difference between this problem and the permutation counting variant.

Solution: dynamic-programming, top-down, $O(nv)$

The given example is too short to find a clear pattern. Let's analyze a slightly more complicated example: paying amount 6 with coins [1, 2, 5]. There are 5 ways to pay the amount:

- 6 = 5 + 1
- 6 = 2 + 2 + 2
- 6 = 2 + 2 + 1 + 1
- 6 = 2 + 1 + 1 + 1 + 1
- 6 = 1 + 1 + 1 + 1 + 1 + 1

Let's sort them in lexicographic order:

- 6 = 1 + 1 + 1 + 1 + 1 + 1
- 6 = 1 + 1 + 1 + 1 + 2
- 6 = 1 + 1 + 2 + 2
- 6 = 1 + 5
- 6 = 2 + 2 + 2

> **Sorting solutions**
>
> Notice the solution sorting trick once again. This is very helpful to extract visually patterns that could be then generated through a recursive algorithm.

We can formulate the following rule that generates these payments:

- Consider coin 1. It can appear in the payment between 0 and 6 times. Consider each option:
  - Do not pay with 1 at all. Count the number of ways to pay 6 with [2, 5]:
    - 6 = 2 + 2 + 2

- Pay with 1 once. Count the number of ways to pay the remaining amount (5) with [2, 5]:
    - 5 = 5
- Pay with 1 twice. Count the number of ways to pay the remaining amount (4) with [2, 5]:
    - 4 = 2 + 2
- Pay with 1 three times. Count the number of ways to pay the remaining amount (3) with [2, 5]:
    - Impossible.
- Pay with 1 four times. Count the number of ways to pay the remaining amount (2) with [2, 5]:
    - 2 = 2
- Pay with 1 five times. Count the number of ways to pay the remaining amount (1) with [2, 5]:
    - Impossible.
- Pay with 1 six times. There is nothing left to pay => 1 + 1 + 1 + 1 + 1 + 1.

We found a rule that allows us to reduce the problem to several smaller subproblems: choose a coin, and use it some number of times to pay a part of the amount; then pay the remaining amount with a smaller set of coins.

If it's not clear yet, let's look at the first two iterations when applying this rule:

Consider coin 1. It can appear in the payment between 0 and 6 times. Consider each option:

- Do not pay with 1 at all. Count the number of ways to pay 6 with [2, 5]:
    - Consider coin 2. It can appear in the payment between 0 and 3 times. Consider each option:
        - Do not pay with 2 at all. Count the number of ways to pay the remaining amount (6) with [5]:
            - Impossible.
        - Pay with 2 once. Count the number of ways to pay the remaining amount (4) with [5]:
            - Impossible.
        - Pay with 2 twice. Count the number of ways to pay the remaining amount (2) with [5]:
            - Impossible.
        - Pay with 2 three times. There is nothing left to pay => 2 + 2 + 2.
- Pay with 1 once. Count the number of ways to pay the remaining amount (5) with [2, 5]:
    - Consider coin 2. It can appear in the payment between 0 and 2 times. Consider each option:
        - Do not pay with 2 at all. Count the number of ways to pay the remaining amount (6) with [5]:
            - 5 = 5
        - Pay with 2 once. Count the number of ways to pay the remaining amount (3) with [5]:

- Impossible.
  - Pay with 2 twice. Count the number of ways to pay the remaining amount (1) with [5]:
    - Impossible.
- Pay with 1 twice. Count the number of ways to pay the remaining amount (4) with [2, 5]:
  - Consider coin 2. It can appear in the payment between 0 and 2 times. Consider each option:
    - Do not pay with 2 at all. Count the number of ways to pay the remaining amount (4) with [5]:
      - Impossible.
    - Pay with 2 once. Count the number of ways to pay the remaining amount (2) with [5]:
      - Impossible.
    - Pay with 2 twice. There is nothing left to pay => 1 + 1 + 2 + 2;
- Pay with 1 three times. Count the number of ways to pay the remaining amount (3) with [2, 5]:
  - Impossible.
- Pay with 1 four times. Count the number of ways to pay the remaining amount (2) with [2, 5]:
  - 2 = 2
- Pay with 1 five times. Count the number of ways to pay the remaining amount (1) with [2, 5]:
  - Impossible.
- Pay with 1 six times. There is nothing left to pay => 1 + 1 + 1 + 1 + 1 + 1.

We can implement this rule using a helper function that takes as parameters the amount left to be paid and the index of the next coin to be considered (assuming coins are stored in a list).

We can see from the examples above that there are a lot of redundant computations, so we cache the results to reduce the time complexity. We will analyze how much after we write the solution.

We can write the solution as:

```python
def count_ways_to_pay(coins, amount):
    @lru_cache
    def count_ways_helper(index, amount):
        # Nothing more left to pay: a single way.
        if amount == 0:
            return 1
        # Invalid payment: we either paid too much so the amount that
        # remains is negative, or we still have something to pay but
        # we ran out of coins.
        if amount < 0 or index == len(coins):
            return 0
```

```
        num_ways = 0
        coin = coins[index]
        # Consider all the possible amounts to pay with the coin:
        for repeats in range(amount // coin + 1):
            payment = coin * repeats
            # Count the ways to pay the rest of the amount.
            num_ways += count_ways_helper(index + 1, amount - payment)
        return num_ways
    return helper(amount)
```

The time complexity is $O(nv)$, where n is the number of coins and v is the amount we have to pay.

4 Number of expressions with a target result

Given a list of integers and a target result, count the number of ways in which we can add + or - operators between the integers such that the expression that is formed is equal to the target result.

Example: Given numbers [1, 2, 2, 3, 1] and target result 3, we can form three expressions:

- 1 + 2 + 2 - 3 + 1 = 3
- 1 + 2 - 2 + 3 - 1 = 3
- 1 - 2 + 2 + 3 - 1 = 3

Therefore the answer is 3.

Clarification questions

Q: What result should be returned if the list contains a single number?
A: No operators can be added in this case, so the only expression that can be formed is the given number itself. Return 1 if the number is equal to the result, 0 otherwise.

Q: What result should be returned if the list contains no numbers?
A: The result should be zero, since no expressions can be formed.

Q: How long can the list be?
A: It may contain up to 30 numbers.

Solution 1: brute-force, $O(2^n)$ time

A straightforward solution is to generate all possible expressions, keep only the ones that are equal to the target result, and count them.

We can generate expressions incrementally, assigning operators one by one. For each operator, we have 2 choices: either use + or -. To generate all expressions, we first use + for the first operator, then continue assigning the other operators recursively; then we revisit the first operator and use - this time, then assign the other operators recursively once more. We apply the same rule to the other operators.

Whenever we form a full expression, we check if its result is equal to the target, and if it is, we count it.

Here is an example of using this method on numbers [1, 2, 3]:

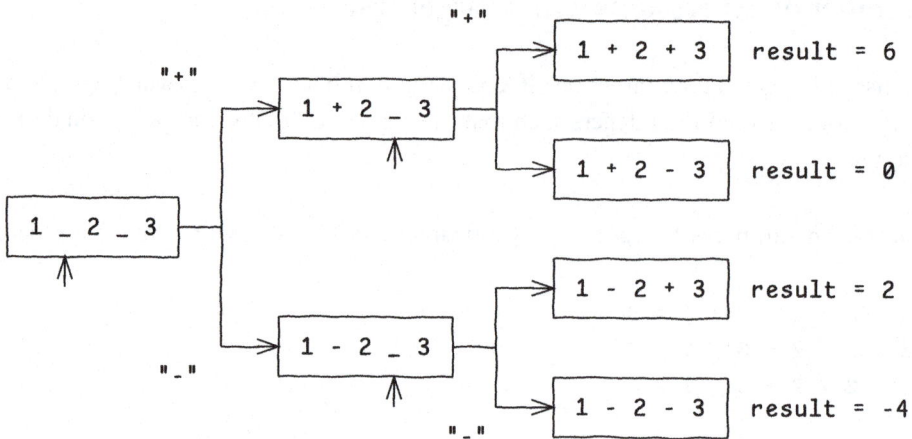

The solution can be implemented as:

```python
def count_expressions(numbers, target_result):
    def count(index, partial_result):
        """
        Counts the number of expressions equal to `target_result`,
        given that the first `index` operators have been assigned,
        thus the left part of the expression is equal to `partial_result`.
        """
        if index == len(numbers):
            # We formed a full expression. Count it if we hit the target.
            if partial_result == target_result:
                return 1
            return 0
        # For the operator before `numbers[index]`, we have two options:
        # Add the `+` sign:
        count_add = count(index + 1, partial_result + numbers[index])
        # Add the `-` sign:
        count_sub = count(index + 1, partial_result - numbers[index])
        # Each option may yield some valid expressions. Sum up the counters.
        return count_add + count_sub
    first_index = 1
    partial_result = numbers[0]
    return count(first_index, partial_result)
```

The complexity is $O(2^n)$, where n = `len(numbers)`. This can be proved by induction: if we increase the input number list length by 1 (by appending a number), the number of steps we make doubles.

The complexity can be also be determined graphically from the tree we have drawn for the example. It is a complete binary tree, where each node represents a step in the execution of the algorithm. The height of the tree is n, thus the number of nodes is $2^n - 1$, which gives $O(2^n)$ steps.

Since we have to handle up to 30 numbers, the brute-force algorithm has to make 1 billion steps, which is too slow.

Solution 2: dynamic programming, top-down, $O(nS)$ time

We can speed up our computation if we notice that we are doing redundant computations. The previous example is too small to see any redundancies, since there are no two expressions with the same sum. Let's consider another example where the list of numbers is [1, 1, 1, 1]:

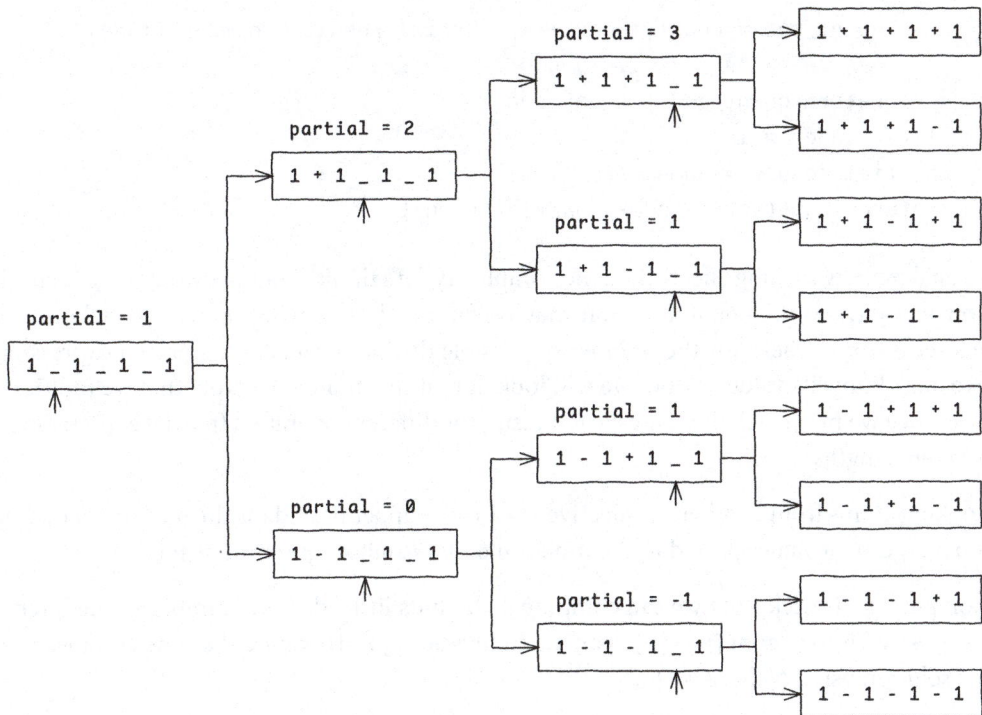

We find two subtrees that are redundant: the prefixes 1 + 1 - 1 and 1 - 1 + 1 have the same partial result 1. Therefore it does not make sense to compute the expression count for subtrees twice, since it is the same.

To avoid redundant computations, we can add a cache for the helper function:

```
from functools import lru_cache


def count_expressions(numbers, target_result):
    @lru_cache(maxsize=None)
    def count(index, partial_result):
        """
        Counts the number of expressions equal to `target_result`,
        given that the first `index` operators have been assigned,
        thus the left part of the expression is equal to `partial_result`.
```

```
    """
    if index == len(numbers):
        # We formed a full expression. Count it if we hit the target.
        if partial_result == target_result:
            return 1
        return 0
    # For the operator before `numbers[index]`, we have two options:
    # Add the `+` sign:
    count_add = count(index + 1, partial_result + numbers[index])
    # Add the `-` sign:
    count_sub = count(index + 1, partial_result - numbers[index])
    # Each option may yield some valid expressions. Sum up the counters.
    return count_add + count_sub
first_index = 1
partial_result = numbers[0]
return count(first_index, partial_result)
```

To analyze how caching affects the time complexity, let's think about the worst-case scenario: how many times the count function may execute without having the result cached. The answer is $n \times s$, where s is the number of possible distinct results of the partial expressions (we don't know its value yet, but we will look at that in a moment). Note that we multiply s by n since we may reach the same partial result for different operators (partial expressions of different lengths).

Looking at this from another perspective, $n \times s$ is the upper bound for the number of distinct input argument values passed to the function count(index, partial_result).

Computing s is tricky, but we can compute its bounds instead. s is a number in the interval $[-S, S]$ with S = sum([abs(x) for x in numbers]). Therefore the time complexity of the solution using caching is $O(nS)$.

This may be an overestimate of the actual number of steps when the input numbers are all large (for example: [1000, 2000, 3000]). For small numbers, it is a tight bound.

> **Thinking about the worst-case scenario and upper bounds**
>
> When it is hard to reason about the complexity of a solution, it is often easier to focus on the worst-case scenario. But sometimes, even analyzing that is difficult. In these cases it may help to think about an upper bound. Upper bounds are useful in practice, especially for capacity planning, since they provide guarantees about the maximum resource usage of a system.

Solution 3: dynamic programming + BFS, bottom-up, $O(nS)$ time

We can rewrite the solution in non-recursive form, using similar expression generation rules.

We start with a simple expression containing only the first number. We then extend this expression with an operator and the next number, in all possible ways, obtaining expressions having two numbers. We store these new expressions in a list. At this point, we can discard the expression containing just one number, and start further expansions from the expressions containing two numbers. We repeat the procedure until we obtain a list of complete expressions.

The problem with this approach is that the memory requirements are very large, since we have to store up to 2^n expressions.

To improve memory efficiency, we do not store the partial expressions, only their results. We can make the storage even more efficient by eliminating duplicate values: we maintain a counter for each partial result; by default it is 1, and we increment it each time we find a new expression having the same result. These counters can be stored in a dictionary, or the Python `collections.Counter` type.

To understand this approach better, consider an example where numbers = [1, 1, 1, 1]. At each step, we compute the dictionary `partial_result_count`, where `partial_result_count[value]` stores the number of expressions formed from `numbers[:index]` having the result equal to `value`.

Here are all the steps performed by the algorithm:

- Initially the only expression is "1". Then `partial_result_count = {1: 1}` (i.e. value 1 can be formed in one way).
- We add the second number to the known expressions, once as "value + 1" and once as "value - 1". We can obtain two possible partial results:
  - 2 from the previous value 1 by adding 1;
  - 0 from the previous value 1 by subtracting 1.
  We update `partial_result_count = {2: 1, 0: 1}`. Note that we keep counters only for values obtained for expressions with 2 numbers.
- We add the third number to the known expressions, once as "value + 1" and once as "value - 1". We can obtain the following partial results:
  - 3 from the previous value 2 by adding 1;
  - 1 from the previous value 0 by adding 1;
  - 1 from the previous value 2 by subtracting 1;
  - -1 from the previous value 0 by subtracting 1.
  We update `partial_result_count = {3: 1, 1: 2, -1: 1}`. We keep counters only for values obtained for expressions with 3 numbers. Note that the counter for value 1 is 2, since there are two possible expressions that generate it. This is the first redundancy encountered so far.
- We add the fourth number to the known expressions, once as "value + 1" and once as "value - 1". We can obtain the following partial results:
  - 4 from the previous value 3 by adding 1;
  - 2 from the previous value 1 by adding 1;
  - 0 from the previous value -1 by adding 1;
  - 2 from the previous value 3 by subtracting 1;
  - 0 from the previous value 1 by subtracting 1;

- -2 from the previous value -1 by subtracting 1.
  We update `partial_result_count = {4: 1, 2: 3, 0: 3, -2: 1}`.
- Since we exhausted all numbers, `partial_result_count` stores the final result count.
  We simply return `partial_result_count[target_result]`.

This solution can be implemented as:

```python
import collections


def count_expressions(numbers, target_result):
    # The offset reached in the list of numbers.
    index = 1
    # partial_result_count[value] = count of expressions formed
    #      from numbers[:index] having the result equal to `value`.
    partial_result_count = collections.Counter({ numbers[0]: 1 })
    while index < len(numbers):
        next_result_count = collections.Counter()
        for prefix_result, count in partial_result_count.items():
            # For each prefix, we extend the expression with
            # + numbers[index] and - numbers[index].
            new_result_add = prefix_result + numbers[index]
            new_result_sub = prefix_result - numbers[index]
            # Propagate the counters to the new expressions.
            next_result_count[new_result_add] += count
            next_result_count[new_result_sub] += count
        # Advance to the next number.
        partial_result_count = next_result_count
        index += 1
    return partial_result_count[target_result]
```

The time complexity is $O(nS)$, since we iterate over n numbers, and at each iteration we process s partial results. As previously discussed, s a number in the interval `[-S, S]` where `S = sum([abs(x) for x in numbers])`.

The space complexity is $O(S)$. This is better than the recursive solution, which had space complexity $O(nS)$, due to the cache. The solution is also likely faster due to the lack of function call overheads.

Unit tests

We propose three unit tests:

The first test handles a few short lists of numbers, for which the expressions can be computed by hand, thus it is easy to verify that the result is correct.

The second test handles the edge case where there is a single number in the list. We check two subcases: one where the number matches the target result, and another one where it does not.

The third test handles large inputs, thus checking if the solution has good performance. In this case, it is too difficult to check the result by hand.

We use instead a very simple input: all numbers equal to one, and target result zero. For this input, the number of expressions having a target result can be computed using combinatorics. To generate expressions with n ones, with n even, and target sum zero, half of the operators must be "-" and the other half must be "+", such that they cancel each other out. The number of such expressions is $\binom{n-1}{n/2}$, since there are $n-1$ operators in an expression, out of which $n/2$ have to be chosen as "-".

The tests can be written as:

```python
class TestCountExpressions(unittest.TestCase):
    def test_1_simple(self):
        self.assertEqual(count_expressions([2, 1, 1], 2), 2)
        self.assertEqual(count_expressions([1, 2, 2, 3, 3], 7), 2)
        self.assertEqual(count_expressions([1, 2, 2, 3, 1], 3), 3)

    def test_2_single_number(self):
        self.assertEqual(count_expressions([3], 2), 0)
        self.assertEqual(count_expressions([3], 3), 1)

    def test_3_perf(self):
        self.assertEqual(count_expressions([1] * 20, 0), math.comb(19, 10))
        self.assertEqual(count_expressions([1] * 30, 0), math.comb(29, 15))
```

5   Partitioning a set into equal-sum parts

Given a set of positive integers, determine if it can be partitioned into two parts having equal sum.

Example 1: `numbers = [2, 3, 5, 6]` can be partitioned into `[2, 6]` and `[3, 5]`, which both have sum 8.

Clarification questions

Q: What result should be returned for the empty set?
A: The set is guaranteed not to be empty.

Q: How large may the set be?
A: Up to 50 elements.

Solution 1: dynamic programming, top-down, $O(nS)$ time

A straightforward brute-force solution is to enumerate all possible subsets `s1`; for each one, compute the complement `s2 = numbers - s1`; then check if `sum(s1) == sum(s2)`.

The problem with this approach is its performance: if there are n numbers, this solution has time complexity $O(n2^n)$, since there are 2^n possible subsets, and computing the sum of each set requires $O(n)$ operations. This is too slow: the algorithm does not scale to the given upper limit of 50 numbers.

Nevertheless, the brute-force idea is useful, since we notice an interesting property: if two subsets `s1` and `s2` form an equal-sum partition, then the following are true:

- `sum(s1) == sum(s2)`;
- `sum(s1) + sum(s2) == sum(numbers)`.

This means that `sum(s1) == sum(s2) == sum(numbers) / 2`. Therefore we can reduce the problem to finding subset `s1` having sum `S = sum(numbers) / 2`.

The search can be formulated using recursion. For the first element of numbers `numbers[0]`, we have two choices:

- Do not include `numbers[0]` into `s1`. Try to form `s1` from `numbers[1:]`, with the target sum `S`.
- Include `numbers[0]` into `s1`. Form the rest of `s1` from `numbers[1:]`, with the target sum `S - numbers[0]`.

Here is an example of the steps we make to solve `numbers = [2, 3, 5, 6]`, with recursion depth shown up to 2:

- Form `s1` from `numbers[0:]` with `target_sum` 8:
    - Try without including `numbers[0] == 2` into `s1`. Form `s1` from `numbers[1:]` with `target_sum` 8:
        - Try without including `numbers[1] == 3` into `s1`. Form `s1` from `numbers[2:]` with `target_sum` 8: ...

- • Try including `numbers[1]` `==` 3 into s1. Form s1 from `numbers[2:]` with target_sum 8 - 3 = 5: ...
- • Try including `numbers[0]` `==` 2 into s1. Form s1 from `numbers[1:]` with target_sum 8 - 2 = 6:
  - • Try without including `numbers[1]` `==` 3 into s1. Form s1 from numbers[2:] with `target_sum` 6: ...
  - • Try including `numbers[1]` `==` 3 into s1. Form s1 from `numbers[2:]` with target_sum 6 - 3 = 3: ...

Let's analyze the time complexity of this solution. Suppose we define a function `find_subset(index, target_sum)` that implements the recursion.

Naively, it would seem that we have to make 2^n calls of `find_subset`, since the recursion depth is n and each call makes 2 deeper calls.

However, the number of possible parameter combinations that can be passed to `find_subset` is only n `*` S (n values for `index` and up to S values for `target_sum`). This means that out of the 2^n calls, many are redundant, so we can cache the results to achieve time complexity of only $O(nS)$.

> **Computing an upper bound for the cache size**
>
> Notice how easy it was to reason about the time complexity once we found an upper bound for the cache size. This is often the most straightforward way to compute not only the time complexity of dynamic programming solutions, but also their memory requirements.

We can implement the solution as:

```python
from functools import lru_cache


def can_partition(numbers):
    @lru_cache(maxsize=None)
    def find_subset(index, target_sum):
        """
        Searches for a subset of numbers[index:]
        having sum target_sum.
        """
        if target_sum == 0:
            # If we hit the target_sum, we found a valid subset.
            return True
        if target_sum < 0 or index >= len(numbers):
            # We either overshot the target sum,
            # or ran out of numbers.
            return False
        number = numbers[index]
        # Search numbers[index+1:], either using the current number
```

```
        # or without using it.
        return (find_subset(index + 1, target_sum - number) or
                find_subset(index + 1, target_sum))


    total = sum(numbers)
    if total % 2:
        # Impossible to split it into subsets of equal sum.
        return False
    return find_subset(0, total // 2)
```

Notice the similarity to the solution of the change-making problem. The main difference is that for the change-making problem, we were allowing the use of each number (a coin) multiple times; for this problem, it can only be used once. To enforce this constraint, the recursive function requires the argument index, in addition to the remaining sum.

Identify similarities and differences between problems

A good way to improve your understanding of dynamic programming problems and their solutions is to think about how they relate to each other, as there are often many similarities between them.

6 Splitting a string without spaces into words

Certain languages, such as Thai or classical Latin, do not use spaces to separate words within sentences. This creates some challenges to text-processing software that has to handle words.

Given a sentence recorded as a string without spaces and a dictionary (a list of words), split the sentence into words. In case multiple results are possible, return any of them.

Example 1: Split sentence "helloworld", given the dictionary ["hello", "goodbye", "world"]. Result: ["hello", "world"].

Example 2: Split sentence "catseatmice", given the dictionary ["cat", "cats", "eat", "mice", "seat"]. Result: ["cats", "eat", "mice"] or ["cat", "seat", "mice"].

Clarification questions

Q: What result should be returned for the empty sentence?
A: The empty list [].

Q: Is it possible that the sentence cannot be split into words?
A: Yes. In such a situation, return None.

Solution 1: dynamic programming, top-down, $O(nw)$ time

This problem is similar to the change-making problem, except that we use strings instead of numbers, and concatenation instead of addition. Instead of paying a target amount, we have to split a sentence into words.

We can start from a side of the sentence, either the start or the end. Let's choose the start. We look at all the words in the dictionary, and check which ones are prefixes of the sentence.

For example, for the sentence "catseatmice", we find two possible prefixes in the dictionary: "cat" and "cats". Since we do not know which one may lead to a correct split, we test both of them. In each case, we remove the prefix, then check if the suffix may be split into valid words. Splitting the suffix is a subproblem of the original problem, so we can solve it with a recursive call of the same algorithm.

Let's sketch how the algorithm works on the example "catseatmice", if the dictionary is ["cat", "cats", "eat", "mice"]:

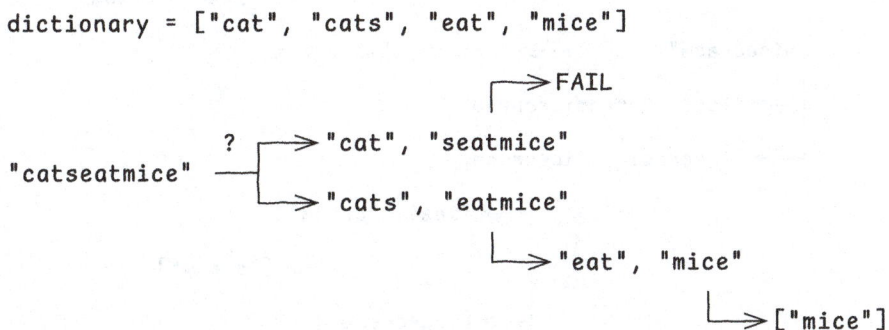

```
dictionary = ["cat", "cats", "eat", "mice"]

                                          ┌──►FAIL
                        ?  ┌──► "cat", "seatmice"
"catseatmice" ──────────┤
                           └──► "cats", "eatmice"
                                          └──►"eat", "mice"
                                                      └──►["mice"]
```

We first find that the word "cat" is a prefix of "catseatmice". We split the string into "cat" and the suffix "seatmice". Now we try to find a way to split the suffix. We do not find any words in the dictionary that are a prefix of "seatmice", so we abandon the search.

Next, we look at the other prefix of "catseatmice": "cats". We split the string into "cats" and the suffix "eatmice".

Now we try to find a way to split the string "eatmice". The only word that is a prefix of this string is "eat". We split the string into "eat" and the suffix "mice", then try to split the suffix.

We find that the suffix "mice" is in the dictionary, so we complete the split as ["mice"].

Walking in reverse over the splits we made, we prepend the prefixes to obtain the solution ["cats", "eat", "mice"].

We can implement this algorithm as:

```python
def split_sentence(dictionary, sentence):
    if not sentence:
        return []
    for word in dictionary:
        if sentence.startswith(word):
            suffix = sentence[len(word):]
            split = split_sentence(dictionary, suffix)
            if split is not None:
                # Any solution works: return the first found.
                return [word] + split
    return None
```

This algorithm has exponential complexity, since it performs redundant computations. This is not obvious from the given example, but noticeable when splitting a sentence like: "ice-creamicecreamicecream" when the dictionary is ["ice", "cream", "icecream"]:

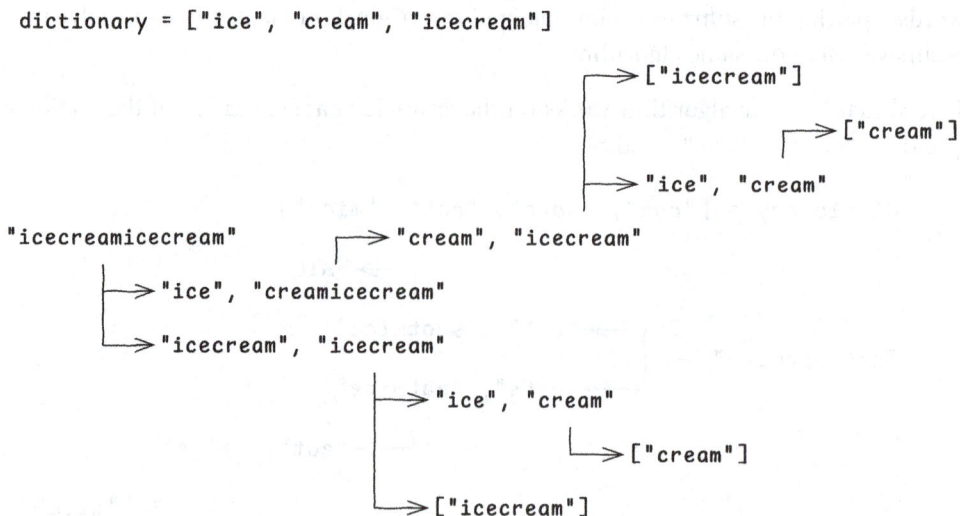

```
dictionary = ["ice", "cream", "icecream"]

                                                      ┌──> ["icecream"]
                                                      │        ┌──> ["cream"]
                                                      ├──> "ice", "cream"

"icecreamicecream"          ┌──> "cream", "icecream"
         ├──> "ice", "creamicecream"
         └──> "icecream", "icecream"
                              ┌──> "ice", "cream"
                              │        └──> ["cream"]
                              └──> ["icecream"]
```

We can see that the suffix `"icecream"` has been split multiple times, so redundant work has been done. This number keeps doubling for each `"icecream"` we add to the input.

We can avoid redundant work by caching the results of the splits:

```python
from functools import lru_cache


def split_sentence(dictionary, sentence):
    @lru_cache(maxsize=None)
    def helper(sentence):
        if not sentence:
            return []
        for word in dictionary:
            if sentence.startswith(word):
                suffix = sentence[len(word):]
                split = helper(suffix)
                if split is not None:
                    # Any solution works: return the first found.
                    return [word] + split
        return None
    return helper(sentence)
```

Just as in the change-making problem solution, we had to write a helper function to avoid caching the `dictionary` parameter, which is not supported by `lru_cache`, since it is mutable.

To analyze the complexity, we need to think about how deep the recursive calls may be, and how much work is done in each call. The depth of the call stack is limited by the length of the string n, since in the worst case we split into short words of 1 character each. In each call we must iterate over the dictionary, in w steps. Overall, the time complexity is $O(nw)$.

Solution 2: dynamic programming + BFS/DFS, bottom-up, $O(nw)$ time

Once we have implemented the top-down solution, we can rewrite it as bottom-up: we start from the empty string, and keep adding words as suffixes in all possible ways that match the sentence:

```python
def split_sentence(dictionary, sentence):
    # splits[prefix] = list of words that form the prefix
    splits = {"": []}
    # prefixes of the sentence that we have not processed yet
    prefixes_to_process = collections.deque([""])
    while prefixes_to_process:
        prefix = prefixes_to_process.popleft()
        if prefix == sentence:
            # Any split works. Return the first found.
            return splits[prefix]
        # Try to extend the prefix with a word matching the sentence.
        for word in dictionary:
```

```
            if sentence[len(prefix):].startswith(word):
                next_prefix = prefix + word
                # Only add the new prefix to be processed if it is not
                # already known, to avoid doing redundant work.
                if next_prefix not in splits:
                    splits[next_prefix] = splits[prefix] + [word]
                    prefixes_to_process.append(next_prefix)
    return None
```

This method is treating the subproblem space as a graph, which is explored in breadth-first order (BFS). We start from the subproblem of extending the prefix "". For each such prefix, we keep expanding using all the possible word suffixes that match the contents of the sentence. The BFS order guarantees that we choose the split with the fewest number of words, although this is not a requirement of the problem; we could have used as well any other search method.

7 The number of binary search trees

Given a list of distinct numbers, count how many distinct binary search trees can be formed to store the numbers.

Example: Given the numbers [1, 2, 3], we can form 5 distinct binary search trees:

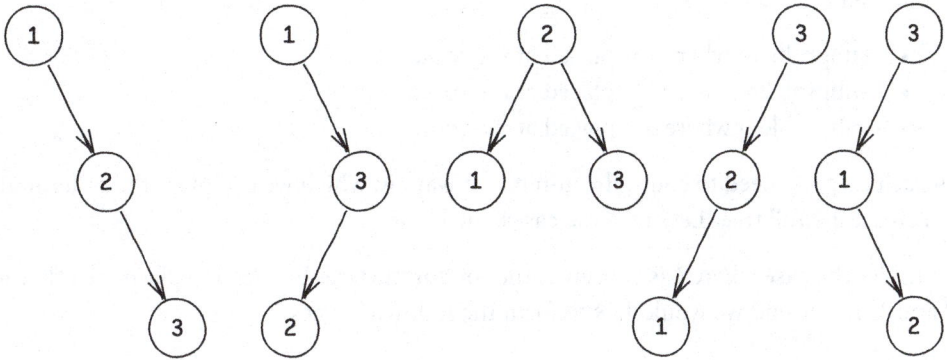

Solution 1: dynamic programming, top-down, $O(n^2)$ time

An important observation we can make is that the number of unique trees does not depend on the values of the numbers in the list, just on their count.

For example, the number of unique binary search trees (BSTs) that can be formed to store [2, 3, 7] is 5 as well:

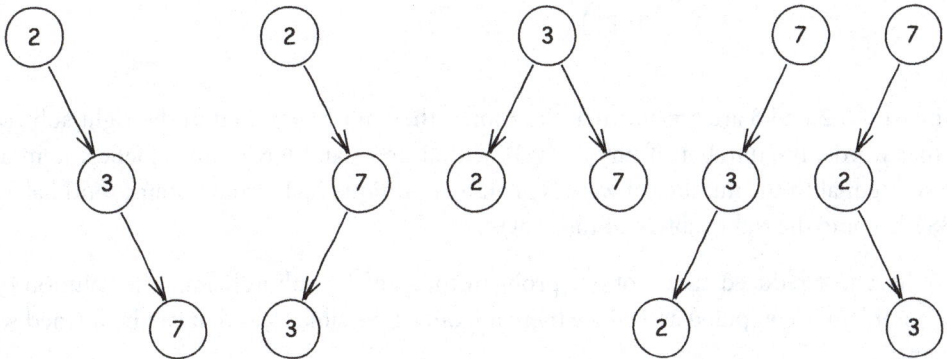

This is easy to prove: suppose that we have an algorithm to generate all the unique binary trees for a list of distinct numbers [a1, a2, ..., an]. For any other list of distinct numbers [b1, b2, ..., bn] with the same length, we can use the same trees and just relabel the nodes: a1 becomes b1, a2 becomes b2 etc. We can relabel the nodes uniquely since we know that there are no duplicates in either list. Thus the number of unique BSTs depends only on the number of elements to be stored.

A second observation that we can make is that we can split the problem into smaller sub-problems if we fix a small piece of the problem that is otherwise variable. Note that this is the same approach we used for the change-making problem (choosing the first coin) and the sentence-splitting problem (choosing the first word).

In case of the BSTs, the natural variable to fix is the item to be placed at the root of the tree.

Consider again the example of items [1, 2, 3]. It is not clear which one should be placed at the root—in fact, any of the numbers is a valid choice. So we split the problem into 3 subproblems:

- a subproblem where 1 is placed at the root;
- a subproblem where 2 is placed at the root;
- a subproblem where 3 is placed at the root.

In each case, we need to count the number of ways in which we can place the other nodes to construct the full tree. Let's take the cases one by one.

Consider the case where 1 is chosen as the root of the tree. We need to place the other items, 2 and 3. In the end we would like to form the following trees:

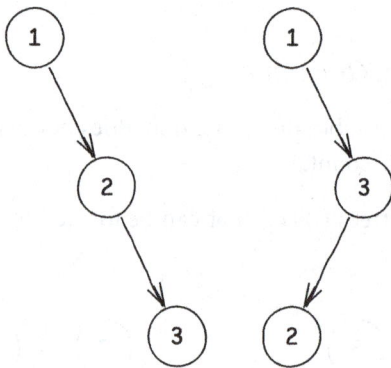

Since both 2 and 3 are greater than the root 1, they must be placed in the right subtree. In other words, the number of unique BSTs with 3 items and having the smallest item at the root is equal to the number of ways we can form unique BSTs from 2 items (and have each BST become the right subtree of the root).

We have just reduced case 1 of our problem to a smaller subproblem. The solution of the subproblem is computed as 2, since there are only 2 possible trees that can be formed with 2 items:

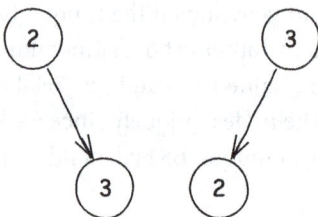

Consider now the case where 2 is chosen as the root of the tree. We need to place the other items, 1 and 3, to form the following trees:

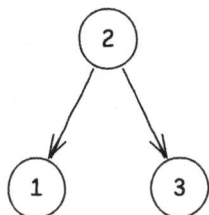

Item 1 must be part of the left subtree of 2, while item 3 must be part of the right subtree. In this case there is only one way to place them. In general, we should count the number of BSTs that can be formed by the items in the left subtree, and the number of BSTs that can be formed by the items in the right subtree. The total number of trees that can be formed is the product of the two numbers (since we can choose any combination to pair them when we construct the full tree).

Finally, consider the case where 3 is chosen as the root of the tree. We need to place items 1 and 2 on the left subtree. This case is symmetrical to the first case (1 fixed at the root), as we can see in the following diagram, so we will not discuss it:

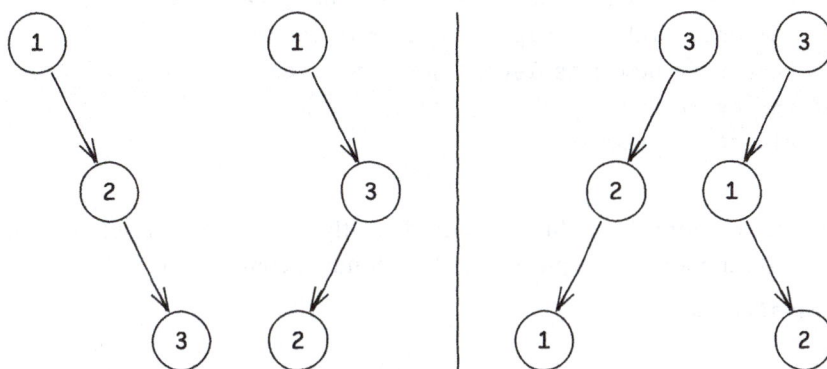

We can now write the implementation of the algorithm. Given that the items are not important for solving the problem, only their count, we can start by defining a helper function that only takes as parameter the number of items:

```python
def count_bsts(items):
    """
    Returns the number of unique binary search trees that
    can be formed using the given items.
    The items must be distinct.
    """
    def helper(num_items):
        ...
    return helper(len(items))
```

The helper function should return 1 if the number of items is 1. Otherwise, it should compute how many trees can be formed by placing at the root one of the items, then return the sum of all these numbers:

```python
def count_bsts(items):
    """
    Returns the number of unique binary search trees that
    can be formed using the given items.
    The items must be distinct.
    """

    def helper(num_items):
        # A single item can be placed in a BST in exactly 1 way:
        # at the root.
        # No items form an empty tree, which is also unique.
        if num_items <= 1:
            return 1
        result = 0
        # Consider all the possible choices of having 1 item at the root,
        # and the rest in the left and right subtrees.
        for num_items_left in range(num_items):
            num_bsts_left = helper(num_items_left)
            num_items_right = num_items - 1 - num_items_left
            num_bsts_right = helper(num_items_right)
            result += num_bsts_left * num_bsts_right
        return result
    return helper(len(items))
```

The final piece we need for solving this problem efficiently is to cache the result of the helper function (to avoid exponential complexity due to redundant computations):

```python
def count_bsts(items):
    """
    Returns the number of unique binary search trees that
    can be formed using the given items.
    The items must be distinct.
    """

    @lru_cache(maxsize=None)
    def helper(num_items):
        # A single item can be placed in a BST in exactly 1 way:
        # at the root.
        # No items form an empty tree, which is also unique.
        if num_items <= 1:
            return 1
        result = 0
        # Consider all the possible choices of item at the root.
        for num_items_left in range(num_items):
```

```
            # Fixing the root, compute how many possible left subtrees
            # we can form.
            num_bsts_left = helper(num_items_left)
            # Now compute how many possible right subtrees
            # we can form.
            num_items_right = num_items - 1 - num_items_left
            num_bsts_right = helper(num_items_right)
            # This is the number of trees having the root fixed to
            # the current item.
            result += num_bsts_left * num_bsts_right
        return result
    return helper(len(items))
```

Since the maximum number of non-cached calls of the function is n (the number of items), and at each call we make $O(n)$ operations, the time complexity of the solution is $O(n^2)$.

8   The maximum-sum subarray

Given an array of integers, find the contiguous subarray having the largest sum. Return its sum.

Example: for [-1, 1, 2, 3, -2], the sum is 6 for the subarray [1, 2, 3].

Clarification questions

Q: What result should be returned for an empty array?
A: The result is 0.

Q: What result should be returned when all elements are negative?
A: The result is the largest negative element, corresponding to a subarray of length 1 containing that element.

Q: What is the maximum length of the input?
A: 1,000,000 elements.

We asked the clarification questions to learn how to handle the edge cases, as well as find out what are the time complexity constraints for the solution. To handle 1 million elements, we must look for an algorithm with time complexity below $O(n^2)$, such as $O(n)$ or $O(n \log n)$.

Solution 1: dynamic programming, $O(n)$ time, $O(n)$ space

The problem involves a search combined with an optimization (maximizing the sub of the subarray), which points to the possibility of a dynamic programming solution. In order to propose such a solution, we need to formulate the problem in terms of smaller subproblems; or the other way around: starting from a smaller subproblem, find a way to extend it to arrive to the original problem.

To find out if this is possible, we first need to understand the properties of the maximum sum subarray. In particular, we are looking for ways of either growing it element by element; or of building it from smaller chunks. Let's analyze some simple examples to find out how this could work.

Firstly, it is clear that when a positive element is part of the maximum-sum subarray, all the positive elements around it should also be part of the maximum-sum subarray. Consider the following example:

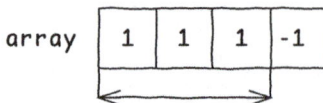

array | 1 | 1 | 1 | -1 |

All of the first three elements form the maximum-sum subarray, with sum 3. It does not make sense to take fewer (such as the first two), since the sum would be suboptimal.

Similarly, it does not make sense to expand to neighboring negative numbers: taking also the fourth element would decrease the sum from 3 to only 2, which is suboptimal.

Does it ever make sense to have negative numbers as part of the solution? Yes, it does, as we can see from the following example:

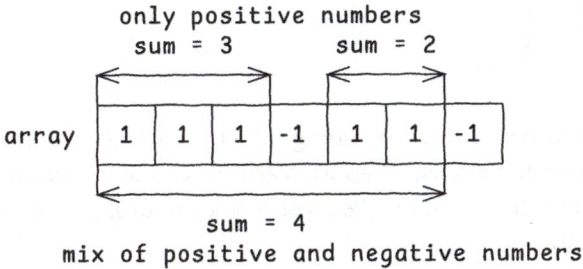

```
              only positive numbers
                sum = 3          sum = 2
              <------------->   <------->
        +-----+-----+-----+-----+-----+-----+-----+
array   |  1  |  1  |  1  | -1  |  1  |  1  | -1  |
        +-----+-----+-----+-----+-----+-----+-----+
        <------------------------------->
                      sum = 4
            mix of positive and negative numbers
```

If we use only positive numbers, the best subarray we can find has sum 3. However, if we allow using the -1 element from the middle, we can pay a small penalty to join the two chunks, to obtain a better sum of 4.

Does it always make sense to pay the penalty to join chunks containing positive numbers? Not when the penalty exceeds the benefit of joining the chunks, as we can see from the following example:

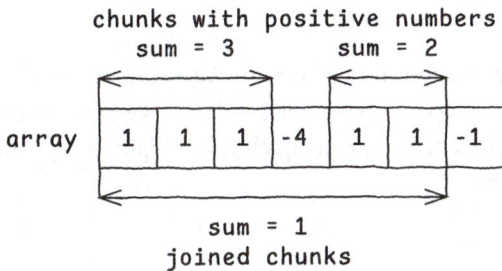

```
            chunks with positive numbers
                sum = 3          sum = 2
              <------------->   <------->
        +-----+-----+-----+-----+-----+-----+-----+
array   |  1  |  1  |  1  | -4  |  1  |  1  | -1  |
        +-----+-----+-----+-----+-----+-----+-----+
        <------------------------------->
                      sum = 1
                   joined chunks
```

Here the negative number is smaller (-4 instead of -1 from before), so joining the chunks does not pay off.

Let's see if we can take advantage of this property when growing the solution element by element. We consider again the example where it makes sense to join the two chunks, and show how the sum of the subarray evolves as we add new elements:

```
              <------------------------------->
        +-----+-----+-----+-----+-----+-----+-----+
array   |  1  |  1  |  1  | -1  |  1  |  1  | -1  |
        +-----+-----+-----+-----+-----+-----+-----+
prefix  |  1  |  2  |  3  |  2  |  3  |  4  |     |
sum     +-----+-----+-----+-----+-----+-----+-----+
```

The prefix sum grows as we add elements from the first chunk, then it decreases slightly when we add the -1 in the middle, after which it increases again as we add elements from the second chunk. So far everything works as expected.

Let's see what is different when the negative element in the middle is heavier:

array	1	1	1	-4	1	1	-1
prefix sum	1	2	3	-1	0	1	

Here we see that the prefix sum goes below zero when adding the -4, after which it grows again but to less than it was before. In other words, when we reach the chunk on the right of -4, we have a prefix with negative sum. It does not make sense to keep it: dropping it and starting a new chunk instead is preferable.

Let's change the example so that the chunk on the right becomes the final solution, to demonstrate the reasoning behind starting a new chunk when the prefix sum is negative:

	sum = 3				sum = 10		
array	1	1	1	-4	5	5	-1
prefix sum	1	2	3	-1	5	10	

Indeed we see that the solution is formed by the chunk on the right with sum 10. Had we included the chunk on the left as well, the sum would have been only 9. We can say that the prefix sum abstracts away the details of the current growing chunk, keeping only what matters: the sum of the numbers in the chunk:

	?		
array	prefix sum: -1	5	5	-1

Here is another example where the sum of the prefix is positive:

	?		
array	prefix sum: 1	5	5	-1

It does not matter what actual elements were part of the prefix. It could have been the following:

	prefix sum: 1				?		
array	1	1	1	-2	5	5	-1

Or it could have been the following:

```
         prefix sum: 1
       ⟨─────────────────⟩   ?
 array │ 1 │ 0 │ 0 │ 0 │ 5 │ 5 │ -1 │
```

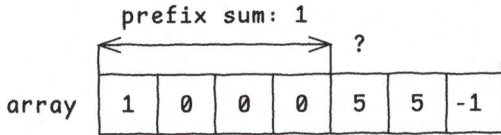

In either case, the outcome is the same: we append 5 to a prefix having sum 1, to obtain a subarray with sum 6.

To summarize what we have learned so far:

- To find the maximum-sum subarray, we can examine smaller chunks of the array;
- A bigger chunk can be formed by appending an item to the chunk preceding it; this should be done only when the sum of the preceding chunk is positive;
- When the sum of the preceding chunk is negative, we should start a new chunk containing a single element;
- The maximum-sum subarray is the chunk with the largest sum.

Let's see a full search running step by step, applying these rules:

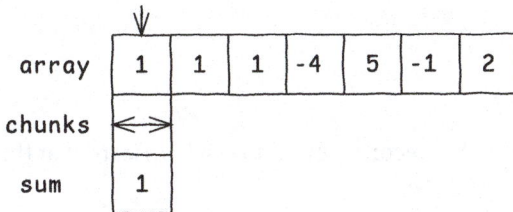

```
              ↓
 array  │ 1 │ 1 │ 1 │ -4 │ 5 │ -1 │ 2 │
 chunks │⟨─⟩│
   sum  │ 1 │
```

We start with a chunk containing the first element, having sum 1.

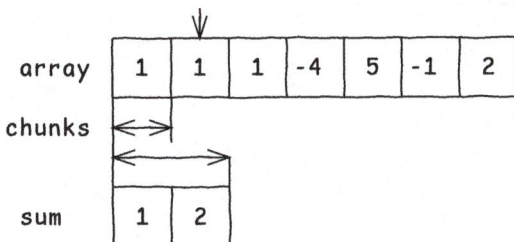

```
                  ↓
 array  │ 1 │ 1 │ 1 │ -4 │ 5 │ -1 │ 2 │
 chunks │⟨─⟩│
        │⟨─────⟩│
   sum  │ 1 │ 2 │
```

Then we examine the second element. Since the previous chunk has positive sum, we grow it to form a new chunk.

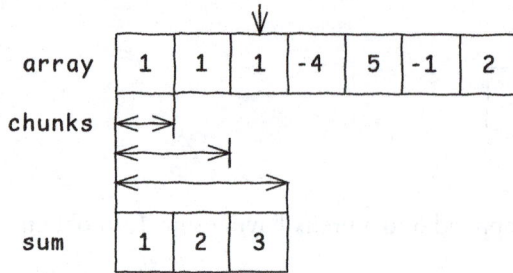

The same for the third element: we grow the chunk again.

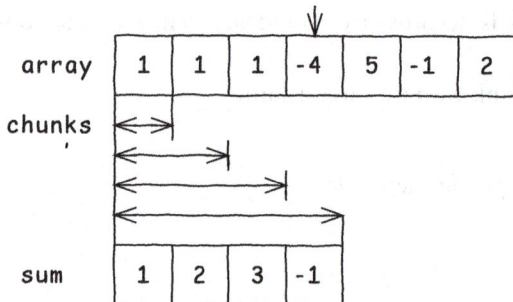

We add element -4 to form a chunk with sum -1. We record it even if we will discard it at the next step.

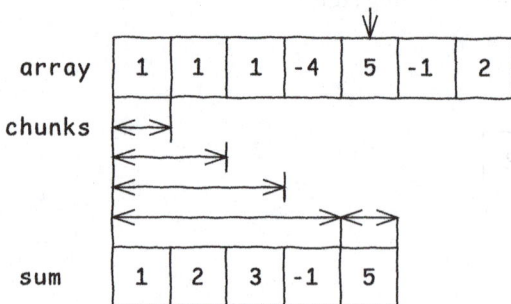

We examine element 5, and we discard the preceding chunk since it has negative sum. We start a new chunk containing only 5.

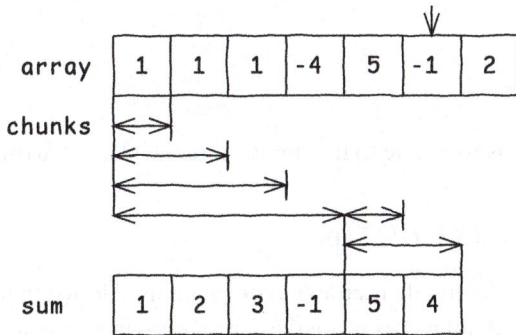

We reach element -1, and we create new chunk with sum 4.

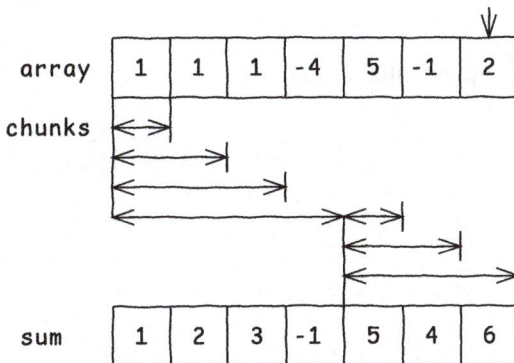

We reach element 2, and we grow the preceding chunk to form a new chunk with sum 6.

We finished examining all the elements of the array. We now simply choose the chunk with the largest sum, which is 6.

This algorithm can be implemented as:

```python
def find_max_sum_subarray(array):
    # chunks[i] = sum of the optimal chunk ending at array[i].
    chunks = []
    for item in array:
        if not chunks:
            # Start a new chunk containing the first element.
            chunks.append(item)
        else:
            if chunks[-1] < 0:
                # Start a new chunk.
                chunk = item
            else:
                # Grow the previous chunk.
                chunk = chunks[-1] + item
            # Record the chunk.
```

```
        chunks.append(chunk)
    # Choose the best chunk.
    return max(chunks) if chunks else 0
```

The running time is linear; the space is linear as well, due to having to store the chunks array.

Solution 2: dynamic programming, $O(n)$ time, $O(1)$ space

We can improve the previous algorithm by reducing its memory requirements. Notice that at each step, only the last element of the array chunks is examined, representing the previous chunk. The only reason to keep the whole array is to compute max(chunks) at the end of the search. We can avoid this by computing a running maximum instead, by keeping track of the best chunk ever seen. Then the chunks array can be replaced with a variable storing the sum of the last chunk, previous_chunk.

This is called Kadane's algorithm, and can be implemented as follows.

```
def find_max_sum_subarray(array):
    # Handle the edge case here to simplify the code handling normal cases.
    if not array:
        return 0
    previous_chunk = -float('inf')
    best_chunk = -float('inf')
    for item in array:
        if previous_chunk < 0:
            # Start a new chunk.
            chunk = item
        else:
            # Grow the previous chunk.
            chunk = previous_chunk + item
        # Update the running maximum.
        best_chunk = max(best_chunk, chunk)
        # Record the chunk.
        previous_chunk = chunk
    return best_chunk
```

Unit tests

For testing, we would first like to cover simple cases to make sure the algorithm works at all. We choose short arrays, so that troubleshooting is easy in case of a bug.

We must also cover the edge cases. We think about not just possible weak points of our implementation, but also cases that could be tricky to handle in general by other implementations, so that we catch regressions in case the code is changed in the future. Some ideas that come to mind are:

- the empty array;

- arrays that contain only negative numbers;
- arrays that contain only positive numbers;
- arrays that contain only zeroes;
- arrays that contain multiple subarrays with positive sum.

Finally, we should have performance tests with large inputs, to benchmark the implementation as well as to catch performance regressions.

The unit tests can be written as:

```python
class TestMaxSumSubarray(unittest.TestCase):
    def test_1_simple(self):
        self.assertEqual(find_max_sum_subarray([-1, 1, 2, 3, -2]), 6)

    def test_2_negative_elements(self):
        self.assertEqual(find_max_sum_subarray([-1, 1, 2, 3, -2, 3]), 7)

    def test_3_local_optimum(self):
        self.assertEqual(find_max_sum_subarray([-1, 1, 2, -9, 4, -1]), 4)
        self.assertEqual(find_max_sum_subarray([-1, 4, -9, 1, 2, -1]), 4)

    def test_4_all_positive(self):
        self.assertEqual(find_max_sum_subarray([1] * 10), 10)

    def test_5_all_negative(self):
        self.assertEqual(find_max_sum_subarray([-1] * 10), -1)

    def test_6_empty_input(self):
        self.assertEqual(find_max_sum_subarray([]), 0)

    def test_7_perf(self):
        self.assertEqual(find_max_sum_subarray([1] * 1000000), 1000000)
```

How much time to spend on unit tests

During an interview you are usually not expected to write a full implementation of the unit tests, unless you are applying for a testing position. However, it is common to be asked for a verbal description of the tests, along with a justification of your reasoning. If on top of that you are able to show that you can write correctly a sample test, or at least mention typical tools you would use such as a unit testing framework or the assertion predicates, this may put you slightly ahead of other candidates.

9   The maximum-product subarray

Given an array of integers, return the product of the contiguous subarray having the largest product.

Example 1: for [2, 3, 4], the product is 24 for the subarray [2, 3, 4].

Example 2: for [-2, 3, 4], the product is 12 for the subarray [3, 4].

Example 3: for [-2, 3, -4], the product is 24 for the subarray [-2, 3, -4].

Clarification questions

Q: What result should be returned for an empty array?
A: The result should be 0.

Q: Can some elements be zero?
A: Yes.

Q: What is the maximum length of the input?
A: 10,000 elements.

Solution 1: greedy, two-pass, $O(n)$ time

Before we try to propose an algorithm, let's consider some examples to identify general cases depending on the sign of the elements in the array.

Firstly, if the array contains only positive numbers, the subarray with the maximum product is the whole array. This is since the numbers are integers, so positive numbers are ≥ 1:

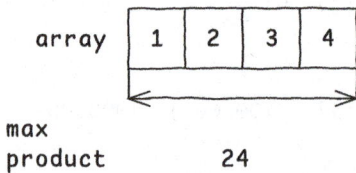

Secondly, we need to handle elements that are 0. Including any such element will cause the product to drop to zero, so we should avoid them. Consider an example:

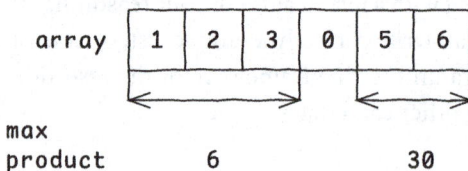

We could say that the 0 acts like a separator: the array can be split into subarrays at any point where it contains a zero. We can search for the solution in the resulting subarrays independently, after which we choose the one having the maximum product as the final solution of the problem.

Finally, we have to handle negative elements. Such elements complicate the search, since they can flip the sign of the product. Let's consider a few examples to understand this effect.

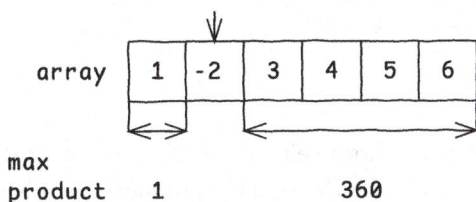

Here we see that we cannot include number -2 in the subarray, since the product will be negative. We have to choose either the left subarray of positive numbers having product 1, or the right subarray with positive numbers having product 360. The solution is the right subarray, since its product is larger.

Let's add a second negative number to see what happens:

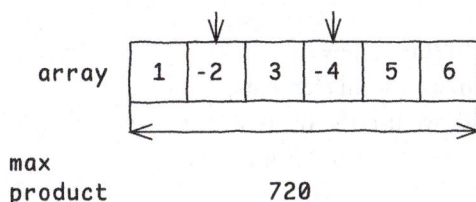

With 2 negative numbers the logic changes: the two negative signs cancel each other out, so we can safely use both in the subarray, to obtain a product of 720.

Let's add a third negative number:

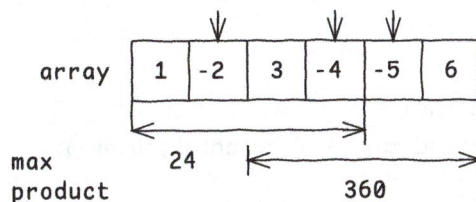

In this case, we can extend the subarray to include two of the negative numbers, so that the signs cancel out. The third negative number cannot be used, since the product would be negative.

We have two choices: either choose the left subarray, ending at -4, or the right subarray, starting after -2. We choose the right one since it has the largest product: 360.

In general, if we have an even number of negative numbers, we can choose the entire array (assuming that it does not contain any zeroes):

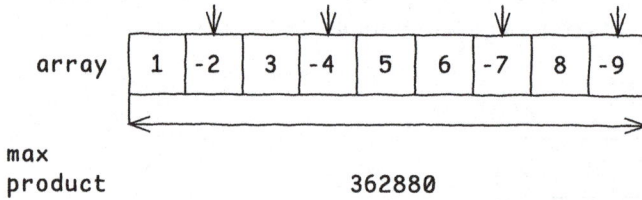

If we have an odd number k of negative numbers, we choose either the left subarray or the right subarray that contains k-1 negatives (note that k-1 is even, so the product is positive):

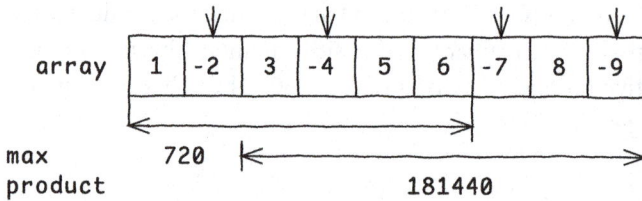

To summarize what we have learned so far:

- Every time we encounter a zero, we have to start a new search;
- If the number of negative numbers is even, we use all elements;
- If the number of negative numbers is odd, we use the biggest of the left or the right subarray that contains an even number of negatives and is maximal.

Let's sketch the implementation:

```python
def find_max_prod_subarray(array):
    def find_non_zero_chunks(array):
        # TODO

    def find_max_prod_in_chunk(chunk):
        # TODO

    max_product = 0
    for chunk in find_non_zero_chunks(array):
        max_product = max(max_product, find_max_prod_in_chunk(chunk))
    return max_product
```

We first extract the chunks of the array that do not contain zeroes. Then we search each chunk for the maximum product subarray. We return the overall maximum.

Let's implement the helper function find_non_zero_chunks:

```python
def find_non_zero_chunks(array):
    chunk = []
    for value in array:
        if value:
            chunk.append(value)
```

```
        elif chunk:
            yield chunk
            chunk = []
    if chunk:
        yield chunk
```

We iterate over the values in the array, appending non-zero values to the current chunk. Each time we find a zero, we yield the current chunk and empty it. We are careful to return the last chunk as well, in case the array does not end with 0 so there are leftover values at the end.

The code can be simplified slightly by removing the need for the final check, by padding the array with a 0 at the end:

```
def find_non_zero_chunks(array):
    chunk = []
    for value in array + [0]:
        if value:
            chunk.append(value)
        elif chunk:
            yield chunk
            chunk = []
```

Let's now implement find_max_prod_in_chunk:

```
def find_max_prod_forward_pass(chunk):
    max_product = 0
    product = 1
    for value in chunk:
        product *= value
        max_product = max(max_product, product)
    return max_product


def find_max_prod_in_chunk(chunk):
    return max(find_max_prod_forward_pass(chunk),
               find_max_prod_forward_pass(chunk[::-1]))
```

To handle the case where there are k negative numbers, with k odd, so that we need to keep only k-1 negatives, we must make two passes over the chunk: one in which we use the first k-1 negatives; and another one in which we use the last k-1 negatives. The two passes are symmetrical, but the logic is otherwise identical.

We take advantage of the symmetry to implement the logic in a single function: find_max_prod_forward_pass. This computes the maximum product by taking the maximum of the running product as we iterate over the array from left to right. In case of k negative numbers with k odd, it will use the first k-1 negatives.

To handle the case of choosing the last k-1 negatives in the chunk, we call the helper function again with the chunk reversed.

Thus we make two passes over the chunk, one in the forward direction by passing chunk, and the other in the reverse direction by passing chunk[::-1] (chunk[::-1] is the chunk reversed).

The way this works can be seen in the following example:

array	1	-2	3	-4	-5	6
product	1	-2	-6	24	-120	-720
max	1	1	1	24	24	24

Notice how keeping track of the maximum product allows us to avoid negative products.

The code is correct also when the number of negatives is even:

array	1	-2	3	-4	-5	-6
product	1	-2	-6	24	-120	720
max	1	1	1	24	24	720

Here is the full implementation:

```python
def find_max_prod_subarray(array):
    def find_non_zero_chunks(array):
        chunk = []
        for value in array + [0]:
            if value:
                chunk.append(value)
            elif chunk:
                yield chunk
                chunk = []

    def find_max_prod_forward_pass(chunk):
        max_product = 0
        product = 1
        for value in chunk:
            product *= value
            max_product = max(max_product, product)
        return max_product

    def find_max_prod_in_chunk(chunk):
        return max(find_max_prod_forward_pass(chunk),
                find_max_prod_forward_pass(chunk[::-1]))
```

```
    max_product = 0
    for chunk in find_non_zero_chunks(array):
        max_product = max(max_product, find_max_prod_in_chunk(chunk))
    return max_product
```

This code can be shortened by removing the split into non-zero chunks, and adding a zero product check in the forward pass:

```
def find_max_prod_subarray(array):
    def find_max_prod_forward_pass(array):
        max_product = 0
        product = 1
        for value in array:
            if not product:
                # Reset the search any time the running product is zero.
                product = value
            else:
                product *= value
            max_product = max(max_product, product)
        return max_product
    return max(find_max_prod_forward_pass(array),
               find_max_prod_forward_pass(array[::-1]))
```

Let's see the forward pass in action on an example:

array	1	2	3	0	-5	-6
product	1	2	6	0	-5	30
max	1	2	6	6	6	30

The new implementation is shorter than before and uses less memory. The disadvantage is that the line `max_product = max(max_product, product)` now has dual purpose:

- It keeps track of the maximum across non-zero chunks;
- It keeps track of the maximum when the running chunk product goes below zero.

This is a tricky point that can make future changes to the code more difficult, so it can be seen as a disadvantage. The longer code may be preferable, even though it is somewhat slower.

Compact and clever code vs. longer but simpler

Making the code compact and clever may come at the expense of readability. Competitive programming resources are often biased towards short and clever implementations. In a software engineering position, these are usually frowned upon, since the code may

> become hard to understand and maintain. Avoid writing the code too cryptic/clever during the interview, since it may be seen as a negative point.

Solution 2: dynamic programming, one-pass, $O(n)$ time

We can convert the greedy solution into a one-pass dynamic programming algorithm using an approach similar to the solution for the maximum-sum subarray: for each index i, we compute the maximum product that can be obtained by a subarray ending at index i. To do that, we consider two choices: either extending the subarray ending at index i-1, or starting a new subarray consisting only of the element at index i.

This approach works well for arrays containing non-negative elements, including zeroes:

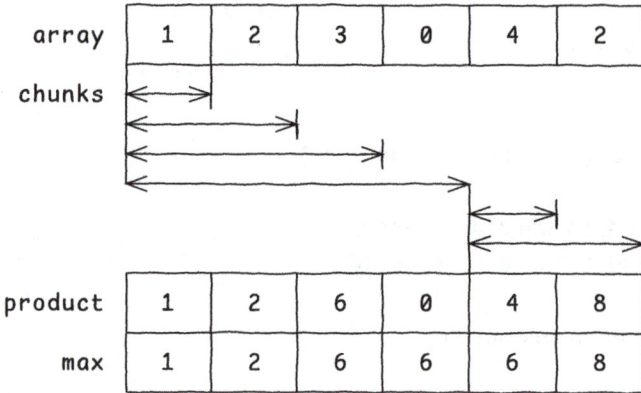

However it fails when there are negative elements:

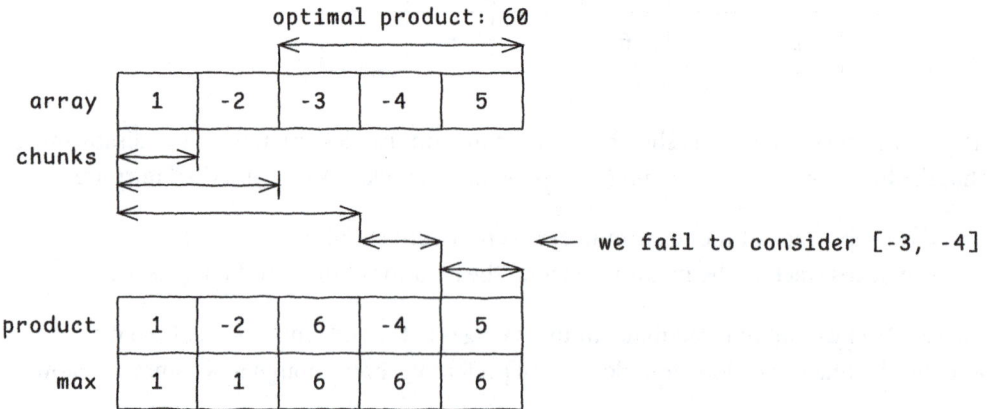

This is because we did not handle a case: when the element at index i is negative, we can also extend an array ending at i-1 that has negative product, to form an array with a positive product. To maximize the product, we must consider the array ending at i-1 that has the *minimum* possible *negative* product.

Therefore we need to keep track of not just the maximum-product subarray ending at index i, but also of the minimum-negative-product subarray.

The maximum-product subarray ending at index i is computed as the best option between the following choices:

- Starting a new subarray containing only the element at index i;
- Extending the maximum-product subarray ending at index i - 1, if it has a positive value and the current value is also positive;
- Extending the minimum-product subarray ending at index i - 1, if it has a negative value and the current value is also negative;
- If not possible to obtain a product > 0, we set it to an invalid value, such as $-\infty$.

The minimum-negative-product subarray ending at index i is computed as the best option between the following choices:

- Starting a new subarray containing only the element at index i;
- Extending the minimum-product subarray ending at index i - 1, if it has a negative value and the current value is positive;
- Extending the maximum-product subarray ending at index i - 1, if it has a positive value and the current value is negative;
- If not possible to obtain a product < 0, we set it to an invalid value, such as ∞.

Here is an example of the strategy in action:

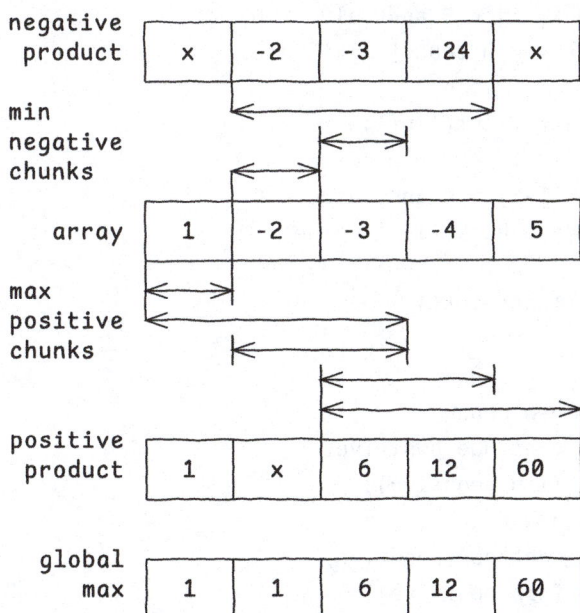

This can be implemented as:

```python
def find_max_prod_subarray(array):
    max_chunk = []
```

```
min_chunk = []
global_max = 0
for value in array:
    # Compute candidates for the max-product subarray
    # ending with the current element:
    # Candidate 1: start new subarray
    max_new_chunk = value
    # Candidate 2: continue positive subarray
    if max_chunk and max_chunk[-1] > 0 and value > 0:
        max_continue_positive = max_chunk[-1] * value
    else:
        max_continue_positive = -float('inf')
    # Candidate 3: flip sign of negative subarray
    if min_chunk and min_chunk[-1] < 0 and value < 0:
        max_flip_negative = min_chunk[-1] * value
    else:
        max_flip_negative = -float('inf')

    # Compute candidates for the min-product subarray
    # ending with the current element:
    # Candidate 1: start new subarray
    min_new_chunk = value
    # Candidate 2: continue negative subarray
    if min_chunk and min_chunk[-1] < 0 and value > 0:
        min_continue_negative = min_chunk[-1] * value
    else:
        min_continue_negative = float('inf')
    # Candidate 3: flip sign of positive subarray
    if max_chunk and max_chunk[-1] > 0 and value < 0:
        min_flip_positive = max_chunk[-1] * value
    else:
        min_flip_positive = float('inf')

    # Choose the best candidate
    max_chunk.append(max(max_new_chunk,
                         max_continue_positive,
                         max_flip_negative))
    min_chunk.append(min(min_new_chunk,
                         min_continue_negative,
                         min_flip_positive))
    global_max = max(global_max, max_chunk[-1])
return global_max
```

Notice how at each step we first compute all the new candidates, then update the max_chunk and the min_chunk arrays. We cannot update max_chunk before computing the candidates for `min_chunk`, as we would compute the wrong value.

The time complexity is linear, and the space complexity is linear as well. We can reduce the space complexity to constant by noticing that we do not need to store the entire array `max_chunk` and `min_chunk`, but only their last value:

```python
def find_max_prod_subarray(array):
    max_chunk = -float('inf')
    min_chunk = float('inf')
    global_max = 0
    for value in array:
        # Compute candidates for the max-product subarray
        # ending with the current element:
        # Candidate 1: start new subarray
        max_new_chunk = value
        # Candidate 2: continue positive subarray
        if max_chunk > 0 and value > 0:
            max_continue_positive = max_chunk * value
        else:
            max_continue_positive = -float('inf')
        # Candidate 3: flip sign of negative subarray
        if min_chunk < 0 and value < 0:
            max_flip_negative = min_chunk * value
        else:
            max_flip_negative = -float('inf')

        # Compute candidates for the min-product subarray
        # ending with the current element:
        # Candidate 1: start new subarray
        min_new_chunk = value
        # Candidate 2: continue negative subarray
        if min_chunk < 0 and value > 0:
            min_continue_negative = min_chunk * value
        else:
            min_continue_negative = float('inf')
        # Candidate 3: flip sign of positive subarray
        if max_chunk > 0 and value < 0:
            min_flip_positive = max_chunk * value
        else:
            min_flip_positive = float('inf')

        # Choose the best candidate
        max_chunk = max(max_new_chunk,
                        max_continue_positive,
                        max_flip_negative)
        min_chunk = min(min_new_chunk,
```

```
                        min_continue_negative,
                        min_flip_positive)
        global_max = max(global_max, max_chunk)
    return global_max
```

This solution is very fast, since it makes a single pass over the array. The disadvantage is that it is much less readable and more error-prone compared to the greedy solution. In a real situation, it should only be used if it is part of a critical path (so its performance matters) and if there are measurements showing that the greedy solution is performing significantly worse.

Unit tests

For testing, we start with simple test cases that cover:

- only positive numbers;
- even count of negative numbers;
- odd count of negative numbers;
- only zero or positive numbers;
- zeroes and positives and negative numbers (odd and even counts)

We also add some performance tests with large inputs, to benchmark the implementation as well as to catch performance regressions.

The unit tests can be written as:

```
class TestMaxProdSubarray(unittest.TestCase):
    def test_1_positives(self):
        self.assertEqual(find_max_prod_subarray([1, 2, 3]), 6)

    def test_2_even_count_negatives(self):
        self.assertEqual(find_max_prod_subarray([1, -2, -3]), 6)
        self.assertEqual(find_max_prod_subarray([1, -2, -3, -4, -5]), 120)

    def test_3_odd_count_negatives(self):
        self.assertEqual(find_max_prod_subarray([1, 2, -3]), 2)
        self.assertEqual(find_max_prod_subarray([1, -2, -3, -4, 5]), 60)

    def test_4_zeroes_positives(self):
        self.assertEqual(find_max_prod_subarray([1, 2, 3, 0, 4, 1]), 6)
        self.assertEqual(find_max_prod_subarray([1, 2, 3, 0, 4, 2]), 8)
        self.assertEqual(find_max_prod_subarray([0]), 0)
        self.assertEqual(find_max_prod_subarray([]), 0)

    def test_5_zeroes_even_count_negatives(self):
        self.assertEqual(find_max_prod_subarray([-2, -2, 0, -5, -1]), 5)
        self.assertEqual(find_max_prod_subarray([-2, -3, 0, -4, -1]), 6)
```

```python
    def test_6_zeroes_odd_count_negatives(self):
        self.assertEqual(find_max_prod_subarray(
                         [-2, -2, 0, -3, -1, -2]), 4)
        self.assertEqual(find_max_prod_subarray(
                         [-2, -2, -2, 0, -3, -2, -2]), 6)

    def test_7_perf(self):
        n = 10000
        self.assertEqual(find_max_prod_subarray([2, 3] * n), 6 ** n)
        self.assertEqual(find_max_prod_subarray([-2, -3] * n), 6 ** n)
        self.assertEqual(find_max_prod_subarray([-2, 3] * n), 6 ** n)
        self.assertEqual(find_max_prod_subarray([-7] + [-2, 3] * n),
                         7 * 6 ** (n - 1))
        self.assertEqual(find_max_prod_subarray([-2, 3] * n + [-7]),
                         7 * 3 * 6 ** (n - 1))
```

10   Shortest pair of subarrays with target sum

Given an array of positive integers and a target sum, find two non-overlapping subarrays such that the sum of the elements of each array is equal to the given target sum, and their total length is minimal. Return their total length.

Example: For [1, 2, 1, 1, 1] and target sum 3, the two subarrays are [1, 2] and [1, 1, 1], with total length 5. There are also two shorter subarrays [1, 2] and [2, 1] having the target sum 3, but they cannot be considered since they overlap.

Clarification questions

Q: What result should be returned for an empty array, or if there is no solution?
A: The result should be 0.

Q: What is the maximum length of the input?
A: 1,000,000 elements.

Solution 1: dynamic programming + sliding window, $O(n)$ time, $O(n)$ space

Let's try to solve an easier problem first: enumerate efficiently all the subarrays having the target sum, regardless of whether they overlap or not.

For arrays of positive numbers, there is an easy solution that involves advancing a sliding window:

- We start with a window containing just the first element of the array:

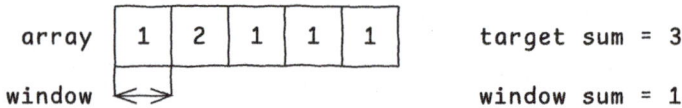

```
array   | 1 | 2 | 1 | 1 | 1 |        target sum = 3

window  |<->|                        window sum = 1
```

- The window sum is smaller than the target sum, so we expand the window to the right:

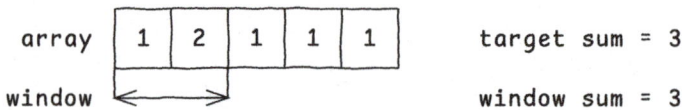

```
array   | 1 | 2 | 1 | 1 | 1 |        target sum = 3

window  |<----->|                    window sum = 3
```

- We found the first subarray. We expand the window to the right again:

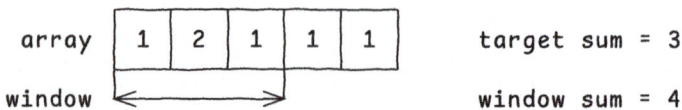

```
array   | 1 | 2 | 1 | 1 | 1 |        target sum = 3

window  |<--------->|                window sum = 4
```

- The window sum is larger than the target sum. We need to shrink the window to reduce its sum. There is no point in shrinking from the right, since we would obtain the window from the previous step. So we shrink from the left, removing the leftmost element:

```
array    | 1 | 2 | 1 | 1 | 1 |        target sum = 3

window       <------->                window sum = 3
```

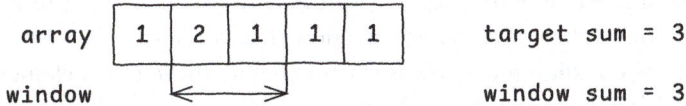

- We found the second subarray. We expand the window to the right again:

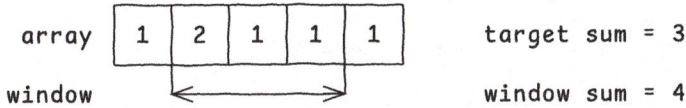

```
array    | 1 | 2 | 1 | 1 | 1 |        target sum = 3

window       <----------->            window sum = 4
```

- The window sum is larger than the target sum, so we shrink from the left, removing the leftmost element:

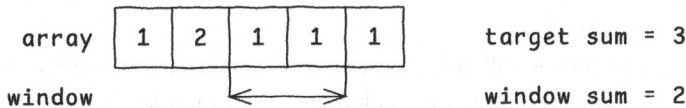

```
array    | 1 | 2 | 1 | 1 | 1 |        target sum = 3

window           <------->            window sum = 2
```

- The window sum is smaller than the target sum, so we expand the window to the right:

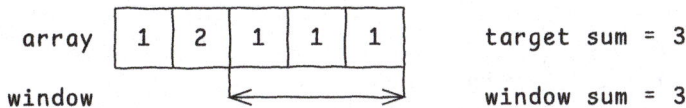

```
array    | 1 | 2 | 1 | 1 | 1 |        target sum = 3

window           <----------->        window sum = 3
```

- We found the third subarray. We expand the window to the right again:

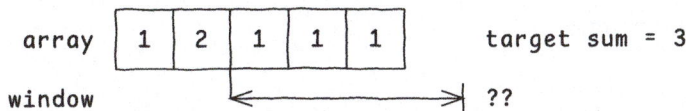

```
array    | 1 | 2 | 1 | 1 | 1 |        target sum = 3

window           <--------------->  ??
```

- We moved past the edge of the array, so we stop the search.

This method enumerates all possible windows that match the target sum. This can be proven in the following way:

- The search ends when the sliding window reaches the end of the array. This means that every element of the array is considered at least once as part of some sliding window.
- Consider a subarray matching the target sum. We want to show that our sliding window algorithm will consider it. From the previous point, it follows that the leftmost element of the subarray is considered at least once as part of some sliding window:

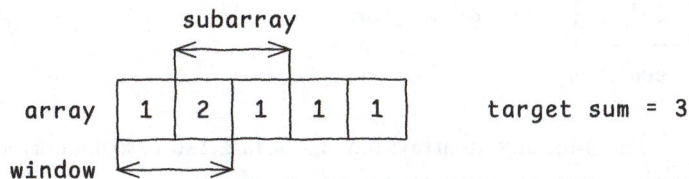

```
             subarray
             <------->

array    | 1 | 2 | 1 | 1 | 1 |        target sum = 3

window <------->
```

- There is at least one sliding window that starts with the leftmost element. This can be shown by contradiction: If there is no sliding window that starts with the leftmost element, it means that the last sliding window is starting before the leftmost element, and ends at the end of the array, then the search ends:

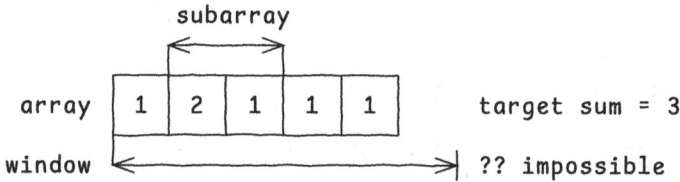

```
              subarray
             ↞──────↠
        ┌───┬───┬───┬───┬───┐
array   │ 1 │ 2 │ 1 │ 1 │ 1 │        target sum = 3
        └───┴───┴───┴───┴───┘
window  ↞──────────────────↠│ ?? impossible
```

But this is impossible, since the sum of this window exceeds the target sum, so we can apply the shrinking rule to advance it. But then it cannot be the last window in the search, so we have a contradiction.

- The right edge of the sliding window will not advance past the rightmost element in the subarray before its left edge reaches the leftmost element. For example, the following is impossible:

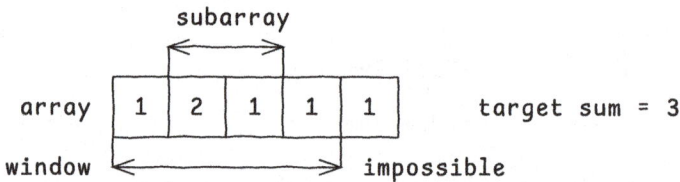

```
              subarray
             ↞──────↠
        ┌───┬───┬───┬───┬───┐
array   │ 1 │ 2 │ 1 │ 1 │ 1 │        target sum = 3
        └───┴───┴───┴───┴───┘
window  ↞──────────↠ impossible
```

This is because the sum of the window exceeds the target sum when its right edge reaches the rightmost element of the subarray:

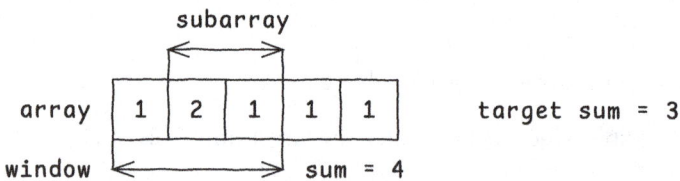

```
              subarray
             ↞──────↠
        ┌───┬───┬───┬───┬───┐
array   │ 1 │ 2 │ 1 │ 1 │ 1 │        target sum = 3
        └───┴───┴───┴───┴───┘
window  ↞──────────↠ sum = 4
```

Thus the next step must be a shrinking, not an expansion. The window will be shrunk until its left edge reaches the leftmost element of the subarray:

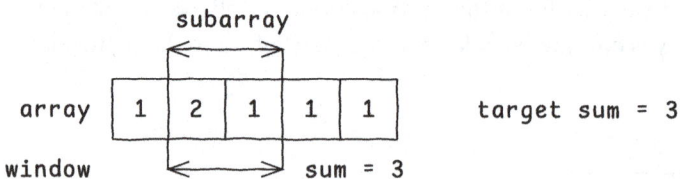

```
              subarray
             ↞──────↠
        ┌───┬───┬───┬───┬───┐
array   │ 1 │ 2 │ 1 │ 1 │ 1 │        target sum = 3
        └───┴───┴───┴───┴───┘
window      ↞──────↠ sum = 3
```

This proves that our solution will not miss any subarrays having the target sum, so it is correct. Note that the method only works if array elements are positive numbers.

> **Sliding window**
>
> There are many problems that can be solved using sliding windows. Not just algorithmic puzzles, but also fundamental problems in computer science, such as reliable data transmission. For example, TCP uses a sliding window to keep track of data that has been sent but not yet acknowledged by the receiver, thus may require retransmission. Understand the concept well: there are many problems for which it can be used to obtain a natural and intuitive solution.

This method can be implemented as:

```python
def enumerate_subarrays_with_sum(array, target_sum):
    window_sum = 0
    left = 0
    for right, value in enumerate(array):
        # Expand to the right.
        window_sum += array[right]
        # Contract from the left.
        while window_sum > target_sum:
            window_sum -= array[left]
            left += 1
        if window_sum == target_sum:
            # Handle subarray.
            print(left, right)
```

Notice how we compute the window sum incrementally in $O(1)$ time at each step, instead of using sum(array[left:right+1]), which takes $O(n)$ time. This allows us to enumerate all windows in linear time.

The overall time complexity is $O(n)$, with n = len(array), since the window expands up to n times and contracts up to n times.

Still, this does not solve our problem, just a part of it. We need to add a few more pieces: applying this to a pair of arrays; ensuring there are no overlaps; and minimizing the total length.

Let's start from minimizing the total length, since it is the easiest next step. We transform the code to solve the following problem: finding the *minimum length* subarray having a target sum.

To do this, we must keep track of the shortest window matching the target sum, when enumerating all possible windows:

```python
def find_shortest_subarray_with_sum(array, target_sum):
    window_sum = 0
    left = 0
    min_length = float('inf')
    for right, value in enumerate(array):
```

```
        # Expand to the right.
        window_sum += array[right]
        # Contract from the left.
        while window_sum > target_sum:
            window_sum -= array[left]
            left += 1
        if window_sum == target_sum:
            # Handle subarray.
            length = right - left + 1
            # Update min_length.
            min_length = min(min_length, length)
    if min_length == float('inf'):
        return 0
    return min_length
```

Let's now extend this solution to find pairs of subarrays having the smallest total length.

We can modify the search such that each time we find a matching window, we sum up its length with the minimum length among matching windows seen previously, and take the minimum overall:

```
    ...
    min_length = float('inf')
    result = float('inf')
    ...
        if window_sum == target_sum:
            # Handle subarray.
            length = right - left + 1
            # Update result.
            result = min(result, length + min_length)
            # Update min_length.
            min_length = min(min_length, length)
    if result == float('inf'):
        return 0
    return result
```

The last point to address is handling subarrays that overlap. The current solution may return overlapping pairs:

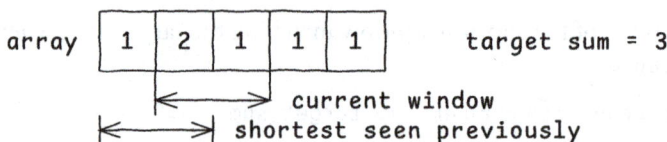

To find the pair of *non-overlapping* subarrays having the smallest total length, we have to sum up the current length with the minimum length seen so far *on the left of the current window*, and take the minimum overall:

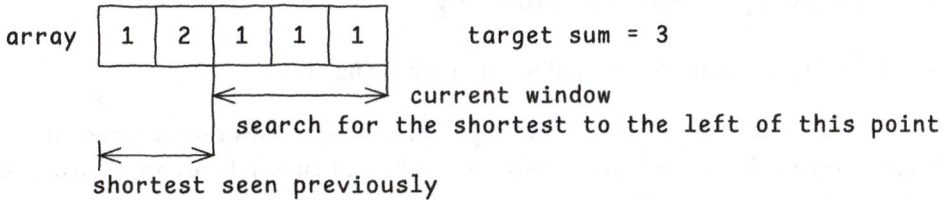

To do this, for each possible left point 0, 1, 2, …, we have to store the length of the shortest array seen with the right edge lower or equal than that left point. We can keep track of it in an array.

This algorithm can be implemented as:

```
def find_shortest_subarray_with_sum(array, target_sum):
    window_sum = 0
    left = 0
    result = float('inf')
    # min_length_up_to[i] = min. length of subarrays with target sum
    #                       having right index <= i.
    min_length_up_to = [float('inf')] * len(arr)
    for right, value in enumerate(array):
        # Propagate min_len_up_to. We may update it later.
        min_length_up_to[right] = min_length_up_to[right - 1]
        # Expand to the right.
        window_sum += array[right]
        # Contract from the left.
        while window_sum > target_sum:
            window_sum -= array[left]
            left += 1
        if window_sum == target_sum:
            # Handle subarray.
            length = right - left + 1
            # Update result.
            result = min(result,
                         min_length_up_to[left - 1] + length)
            # Update min_length_up_to[right].
            min_length_up_to[right] = min(min_length_up_to[right],
                                          length)
    if result == float('inf'):
        return 0
    return result
```

The time complexity is $O(n)$ and the space complexity is $O(n)$ as well.

11   Longest palindromic substring

Given a string s, find the longest palindromic substring of s.

Example: for s = "xabaycddcz", the longest palindromic substring is "cddc" of length 4. There is also another palindromic substring "aba", but that is not the correct answer since it is shorter, having only length 3.

Clarification questions

Q: When there are multiple palindromic substrings of the same length, which one should be returned?
A: Any of them.

Q: Are we looking for palindromes of both odd lengths and even lengths?
A: Yes, both types of palindromes are possible.

Q: Suppose that no palindromic substring of length at least 2 exists. Is a substring of length 1 (i.e. a single character) a valid palindrome?
A: Yes.

Q: What answer should be returned when the input is the empty string?
A: The result should be the empty string.

Q: What is the maximum length of the input string?
A: Most inputs will have no more than a few hundred characters, but it would be great to be able to handle up to 10,000 characters.

We asked the clarification questions to learn how to handle the edge cases, as well as find out what are the time complexity constraints for the solution. For inputs of up to a few hundred characters, an $O(n^2)$ algorithm will work, and even $O(n^3)$ might be acceptable. However, to handle 10k characters, we should look for an algorithm with time complexity faster than $O(n^2)$.

Solution 1: brute force, $O(n^3)$

Let's consider first a straightforward, but naive solution that we can try to optimize later. The idea is to split the problem into two simpler subproblems: searching for the substring and checking if a substring is palindromic.

Checking if a string is a palindrome

Let's first think about how we can check if a string is a palindrome. Essentially, we need to check if it is symmetrical. There are two cases:

The string has an odd length:

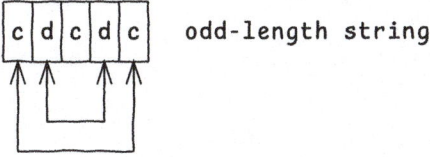

odd-length string

In this case we ignore the middle character, and check if every other character is equal to its mirror. Alternatively, we can consider the middle character as its own mirror to avoid having to give it special treatment.

The other case is when the string has even length:

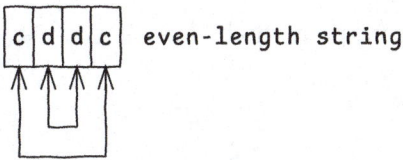

even-length string

In this case there is no middle character. We need to check for every character if it is equal to its mirror.

In both cases we need a helper function that given the index of a character, computes the index of the mirror character. Let's call this function `mirror`. Then the check for the palindrome property can be written as:

```python
def is_palindrome(s):
    for i in range(len(s) / 2):
        if s[mirror(i)] != s[i]:
            return False
    return True
```

Let's now see how we can write the `mirror` function. We can take advantage of the negative indexing in Python, which wraps around: the mirror of `s[0]` is `s[-1]`. Let's look at an example to see how we can extend this to the other indices:

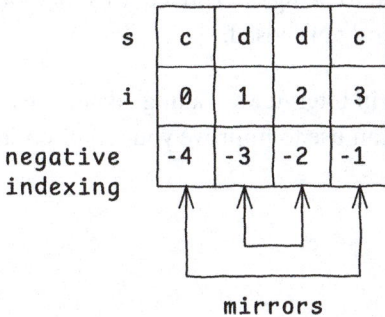

mirrors

We can take as reference `i = 0`, for which the mirror is `-1`. Any time `i` advances by 1, the mirror index has to decrease by 1. Therefore we can compute `mirror(i) = -(i + 1)`.

This formula applies to palindromes with odd length as well:

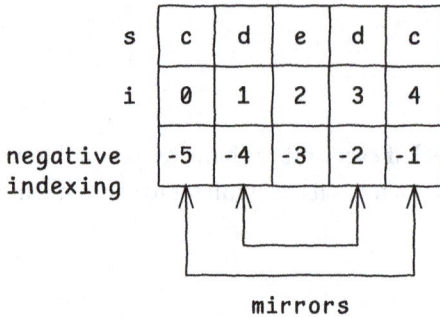

mirrors

Therefore, we can write the complete palindrome property check as:

```python
def is_palindrome(s):
    def mirror(i):
        return -(i + 1)

    for i in range(len(s) / 2):
        if s[mirror(i)] != s[i]:
            return False
    return True
```

Checking if a string is a palindrome: a faster way

Another way of checking if a string is a palindrome is to check if it is equal to its reverse. Reversing a string s can be written in Python as s[::-1]. We can use this to implement a much simpler check:

```python
def is_palindrome(s):
    return s == s[::-1]
```

Due to the way Python uses slices, as well as to the fact that the comparison executes in machine code (as part of the Python runtime) as opposed to being interpreted, this method has better performance than the solution we have previously proposed.

Since this code is also quick to write, it is an useful trick in interviews. Taking advantage of it can shave off a few minutes off your answer, that you can use to improve your solution in other ways.

Putting it all together

Let's now look at how we can find the *longest* palindromic substring.

Suppose that we work on the following input, that contains three palindromic substrings:

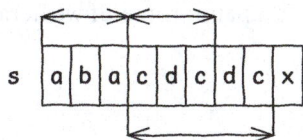

The first method that comes to mind is to iterate over all substrings using two indices `left` and `right`:

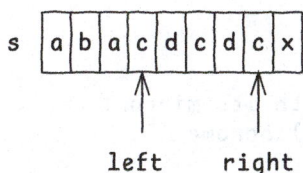

For each substring, we call the `is_palindrome` helper to check if it's a palindrome. If it is, we need to check if it is longer than the one found so far.

The search can be written as:

```python
def longest_palindrome(s):
    best = ''
    for left in range(len(s)):
        for right in range(left, len(s)):
            substring = s[left:right+1]
            if is_palindrome(substring) and len(substring) > len(best):
                best = substring
    return best
```

The time complexity of iterating over substrings is $O(n^2)$. Additionally, the `is_palindrome` helper has $O(n)$ complexity, so the overall time complexity is $O(n^3)$. This answer is a bit slow given the expected size of the inputs.

Solution 2: dynamic programming, $O(n^2)$

The reason why the naive solution is slow is that it performs too many character comparisons: $O(n^3)$.

Note that $O(n^2)$ comparisons are sufficient to cover all the possible pairs of characters in the string; anything beyond this number must include redundant comparisons. This is a signal that the complexity could be reduced by eliminating some of the redundancies.

The idea behind the dynamic programming solution is to reorganize the search for palindromes in a way that we avoid redundant comparisons, by reusing previously computed results.

To perform fewer comparisons, we could change the palindrome property check to make it incremental. To achieve this, we must start from the center instead of the edge.

Consider as an example the test for checking if "cdeedc" is a palindrome. If we iterate over the string from the center, the steps look like this:

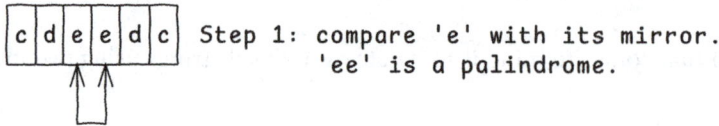

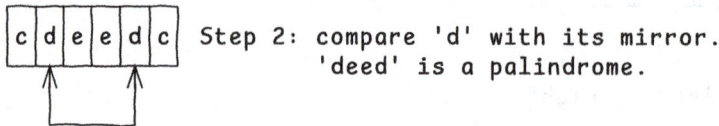

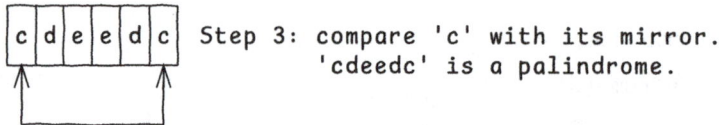

```
c d e e d c    Step 1: compare 'e' with its mirror.
                       'ee' is a palindrome.
```

```
c d e e d c    Step 2: compare 'd' with its mirror.
                       'deed' is a palindrome.
```

```
c d e e d c    Step 3: compare 'c' with its mirror.
                       'cdeedc' is a palindrome.
```

Notice that we computed not just that "cdeedc" is a palindrome, but also the same property for all its smaller substrings that have the same center. This is the key for reducing the time complexity of the solution.

To iterate over all substrings, we no longer use two pointers `left` and `right`. Instead, we use a pointer called `center`. For each value of the center, we expand symmetrically to the left and right as long as the substring is a palindrome:

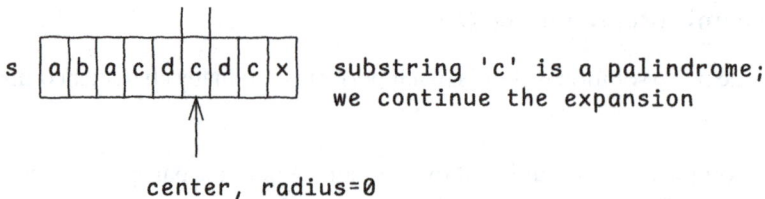

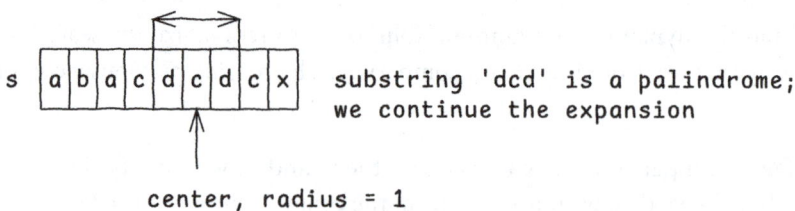

```
s  a b a c d c d c x    substring 'c' is a palindrome;
                        we continue the expansion

      center, radius=0
```

```
s  a b a c d c d c x    substring 'dcd' is a palindrome;
                        we continue the expansion

      center, radius = 1
```

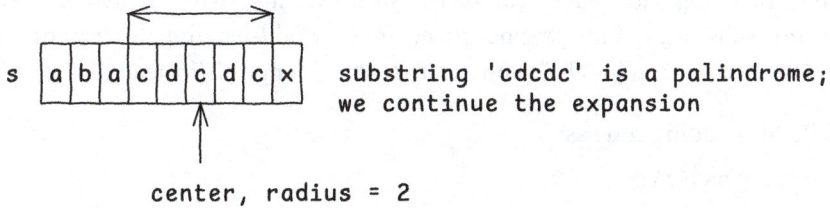

s | a | b | a | c | d | c | d | c | x   substring 'cdcdc' is a palindrome;
we continue the expansion

center, radius = 2

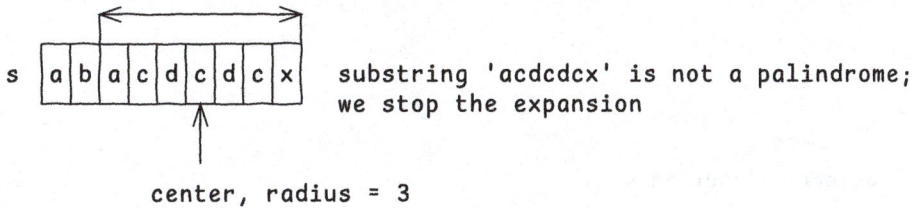

s | a | b | a | c | d | c | d | c | x   substring 'acdcdcx' is not a palindrome;
we stop the expansion

center, radius = 3

The algorithm for searching the longest odd-length palindromic substring can be written as:

```python
def longest_palindrome(s):
    best = ''
    for center in range(len(s)):
        # Expand symetrically as long as the palindrome property holds
        left = center
        right = center
        while left >= 0 and right < len(s) and s[left] == s[right]:
            left -= 1
            right += 1
        # The last move broke the palindrome property, undo it
        left += 1
        right -= 1
        palindrome = s[left:right+1]
        # Record the palindrome if longest
        if len(palindrome) > len(best):
            best = palindrome
    return best
```

It is easy to see that the time complexity is $O(n^2)$.

The problem with this code is that implements the search only for odd-length substrings, not for even lengths. There are a lot of details that need to be adapted for even lengths (for example, the notion of center is ill-defined), so changing the code to handle both cases is not straightforward.

An option is to write two different functions, one handling odd lengths, the other handling even lengths.

Another option is to transform the input string in such a way that any palindromic substring has odd length. This can be done by adding an additional guard character between all characters.

For example, the string "abacdddc" can be transformed into "a!b!a!c!d!d!c". Note that all palindromic substrings of the original string are now odd-length palindromes: "a!b!a" has length 5 (instead of 3 as in "aba") and "c!d!d!c" has length 7 (instead of 4 as in "cddc").

We can write the padding code as:

```python
def palindrome_pad(s):
    """
    Transforms a string such that all palindrome substrings have odd length:
    * 'aa' -> 'a!a'
    * 'abba' -> 'a!b!b!a'
    * 'aba' -> 'a!b!a'
    """
    assert '!' not in s
    return '!'.join(s)
```

The reverse transformation that recovers the initial string is trivial:

```python
def palindrome_unpad(padded):
    return padded.replace('!', '')
```

We also need a helper function that computes the length of the unpadded palindrome, so that we can compare the candidate with the best:

```python
def unpadded_length(padded):
    if not padded:
        return 0
    if padded[0] == '!':
        return (len(padded) - 1) / 2
    return (len(padded) + 1) / 2
```

The final solution:

```python
def longest_palindrome(s):
    s = palindrome_pad(s)
    best = ''
    for center in range(len(s)):
        # Expand symmetrically as long as the palindrome property holds
        left = center
        right = center
        while left >= 0 and right < len(s) and s[left] == s[right]:
            left -= 1
            right += 1
        # The last move broke the palindrome property, undo it
        left += 1
        right -= 1
        palindrome = s[left:right+1]
        # Record the palindrome if longest
```

```
      if unpadded_size(palindrome) > unpadded_size(best):
          best = palindrome
  return palindrome_unpad(best)
```

> **Two tricks for handling palindromes**
>
> In this solution, we have seen two tricks that help when dealing with palindromes: testing the palindrome property with s == s[::-1]; and adding a guard character to transform the palindrome so that it has odd length.

Solution 3: dynamic programming, $O(n)$

There is a further optimization to the solution, called Manacher's algorithm. The intuition behind it is to eliminate redundant expansion steps when the current center is inside a bigger palindrome identified previously:

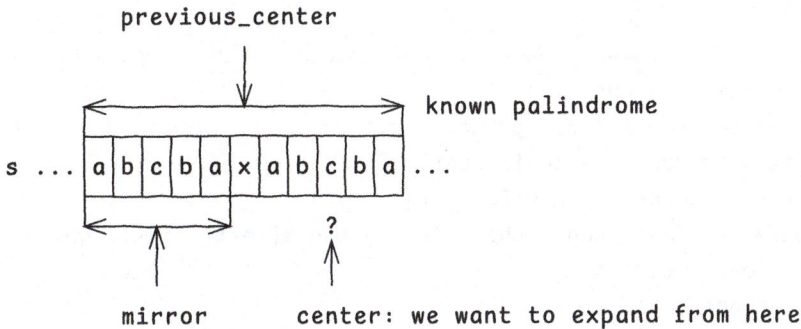

The substring "abcba" on the left is equal to the one we are currently expanding; redoing the expansion steps up to length 5 is redundant, so we can skip them.

We can do that by storing the expansion radius computed for the centers from which we expanded so far:

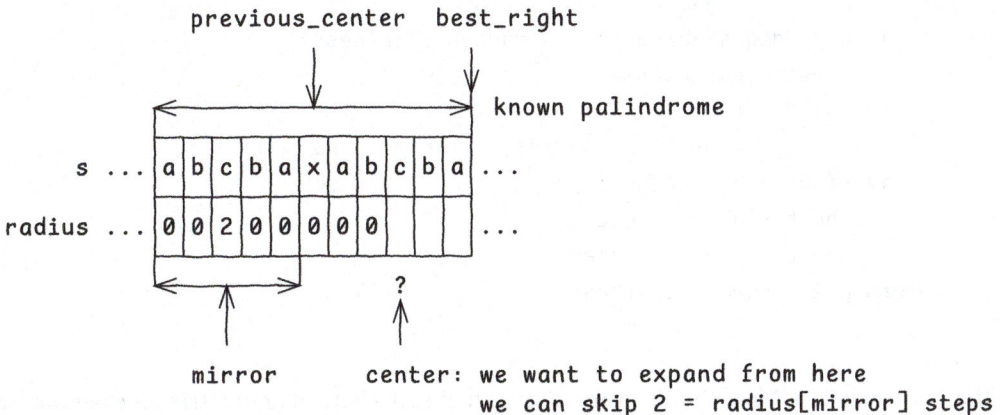

This can be implemented as:

```python
def longest_palindrome(s):
    s = palindrome_pad(s)
    best = ''
    best_right = -1
    best_center = -1
    # radius[center] = best expansion radius found for that center
    radius = [0] * len(s)
    for center in range(len(s)):
        if center <= best_right:
            # Manacher's optimization:
            # The new center is inside a bigger palindrome expansion
            # from earlier. We can skip the first steps of the expansion,
            # since they are equivalent to what we have already computed
            # for the center's mirror.
            mirror = best_center - (center - best_center)
            radius[center] = min(best_right - center, radius[mirror])
        else:
            # Normal case when we do not have any prior knowledge
            radius[center] = 1
        # Expand symetrically as long as the palindrome property holds
        left = center - radius[center]
        right = center + radius[center]
        while left >= 0 and right < len(s) and s[left] == s[right]:
            left -= 1
            right += 1
            radius[center] += 1
        # The last move broke the palindrome property, undo it
        left += 1
        right -= 1
        radius[center] -= 1
        palindrome = s[left:right+1]
        # Record the palindrome if longest
        if unpadded_size(pali) > unpadded_size(best):
            best = palindrome
        # Manacher's optimization:
        # Keep track of the rightmost palindrome seen so far
        if right > best_right:
            best_right = right
            best_center = center
    return palindrome_unpad(best)
```

The consequence of Manacher's optimization is that each element of the string is examined at most once during the inner expansion loop, over the entire execution of the algorithm. This is because there are two cases:

- Either the current center is inside a bigger palindrome seen earlier, in which case it has been examined once before and it is now skipped;
- Or the current center has not been examined before since no palindrome has expanded to this point.

This brings the time complexity to $O(n)$, even if there are two nested loops.

Manacher's optimization is not likely to come up during an interview due to its complexity. Still, it is good to be aware of its existence.

Unit tests

For testing, we would first like to cover simple, normal cases to make sure the algorithm works at all. For this it makes sense to choose short strings that contain a palindrome among other characters, such as "XabaY" or "XabbaY". The inputs should be short so that troubleshooting is easy in case of a bug.

Then we should cover edge cases. We should think about not just possible weak points of our implementation, but also cases that could be tricky to handle in general by other implementations. This is to catch regressions in case the code is changed in the future. Some ideas that come to mind are:

- the empty string "";
- non-empty strings that do not contain a palindrome with length at least 2, such as "abc";
- the whole string being a palindrome, such as "aba", to catch possible off-by-one errors;
- strings containing two palindromes of equal length;
- strings containing two palindromes of different lengths.

Finally, we should write performance tests with longer strings, to benchmark the implementation as well as to catch performance regressions. A simple test can consist of just a single, long palindrome. A more complex test can use multiple long palindromes, possibly of varying lengths. We can generate long palindromes either by repeating a short pattern, such as "aaaaa" and "abababa"; or by mirroring a long random string.

The unit tests can be written as:

```python
class TestLongestPalindrome(unittest.TestCase):
    def test_1_odd_length(self):
        self.assertEqual(longest_palindrome('abaX'), 'aba')
        self.assertEqual(longest_palindrome('Xaba'), 'aba')
        self.assertEqual(longest_palindrome('XabaY'), 'aba')

    def test_2_even_length(self):
        self.assertEqual(longest_palindrome('abbaX'), 'abba')
        self.assertEqual(longest_palindrome('Xabba'), 'abba')
        self.assertEqual(longest_palindrome('XabbaY'), 'abba')

    def test_3_single_char(self):
```

```python
        self.assertIn(longest_palindrome('abc'), ['a', 'b', 'c'])

    def test_4_full_string(self):
        self.assertEqual(longest_palindrome('aba'), 'aba')
        self.assertEqual(longest_palindrome('abba'), 'abba')

    def test_5_empty_string(self):
        self.assertEqual(longest_palindrome(''), '')

    def test_6_two_solutions(self):
        self.assertIn(longest_palindrome('XabaYcbcZ'), ['aba', 'cbc'])

    def test_7_perf_simple(self):
        chunk = 'abba'
        max_len = 10000
        s = 'X' + (chunk * max_len) + 'Y'
        self.assertEqual(longest_palindrome(s), chunk * max_len)

    def test_8_perf_stress(self):
        chunk = 'abba'
        max_len = 300
        s = ''.join(str(i * 1337) + chunk * i for i in range(max_len + 1))
        self.assertEqual(longest_palindrome(s), chunk * max_len)
```

12 Longest valid parentheses substring

Given a string s that contains only the '{' and '}' characters, return the length of the longest substring of correctly closed parentheses.

Example: for s = "{}{{}}{", the longest valid parentheses substring is "{}{{}}" of length 6.

Clarification questions

Q: How large can the string be?
A: Up to 10,000 characters.

Q: What answer should be returned when the input is the empty string?
A: The result should be 0.

Solution 1: dynamic programming, bottom-up, $O(n)$

Let's first think about the structure of valid parentheses strings, to see if there are any properties we can use in our advantage. Specifically, we are interested in anything that can help us reduce the problem to smaller subproblems—or the other way around: building valid parentheses strings incrementally starting from smaller ones.

The smallest valid parentheses string is the pair:

pair

We can build a longer valid parentheses string by appending another pair:

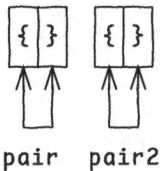

pair   pair2

In general, we can build a longer valid parentheses string by appending another valid parentheses string:

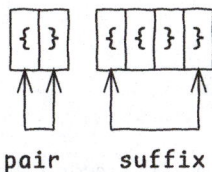

pair   suffix

We can do the same by prepending a valid parentheses string:

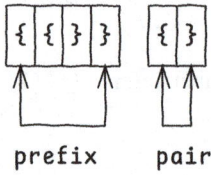

prefix   pair

Prepending or appending are equivalent. We may use one or the other depending on the direction we use to build the string (left to right or right to left).

We can also build a longer valid parentheses string by inserting a pair inside the outer pair:

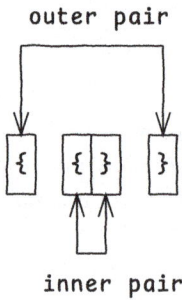

outer pair

inner pair

In general, we can insert any valid parentheses substring inside a pair:

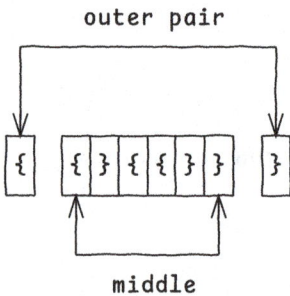

outer pair

middle

These operations are sufficient to build any valid parentheses substring.

For example, let's see how we can apply them incrementally to s = "{}{{}}{".

We look at each character from s, starting from the left:

No valid substring can be formed with the first character. Let's add the second character:

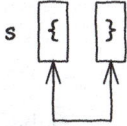

Since the second character is '}', we look for a match to its left to form a pair. We obtain a valid substring of length 2. We continue by adding the third character:

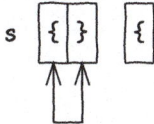

No new valid substring can be formed, since '{' cannot match anything on its left. We add the fourth character:

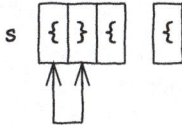

Once again, no new valid substring can be formed, since '{' cannot match anything on its left. We add the fifth character:

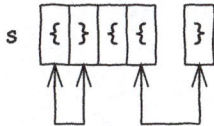

Since the new character is '}', we look for a match to the left to form a pair. We form another valid substring of length 2. We continue by adding the sixth character:

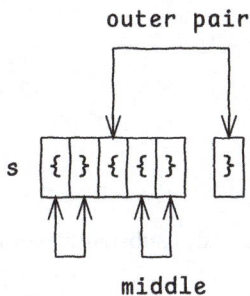

Since the new character is '}', we look for a match to the left to form a pair. There is no '{' behind it, so we cannot form a simple pair.

Nevertheless, we can try applying the outer pair strategy. We see that there is a valid substring of length 2 behind it "{}". We try to use it as the middle substring, and embed it into an outer pair. We succeed, since the character before the middle substring is '{', which allows us to form an outer pair.

Naively, one would think that we formed a valid substring of length 4. However, before this substring, there is a valid substring prefix:

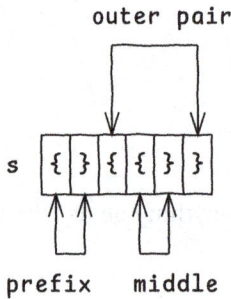

```
              outer pair
             ┌────────┐
             │        │
             ▼        ▼
    s  │ { │ } │ { │ { │ } │ } │
         ▲   ▲   ▲   ▲
         └───┘   └───┘
       prefix    middle
```

Thus we can apply the appending rule to form a longer valid substring:

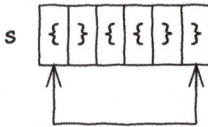

```
    s  │ { │ } │ { │ { │ } │ } │
         ▲               ▲
         └───────────────┘
```

This is the maximal valid substring that can be obtained so far. We can now add the last character:

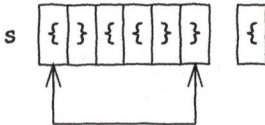

```
    s  │ { │ } │ { │ { │ } │ } │   │ { │
         ▲               ▲
         └───────────────┘
```

This character cannot be matched with anything, so the longest valid substring overall is 6.

Based on this example, we can design the algorithm that solves the problem. We process the input string s from left to right, character by character.

To advance from one index to the next, we try to find the following pattern:

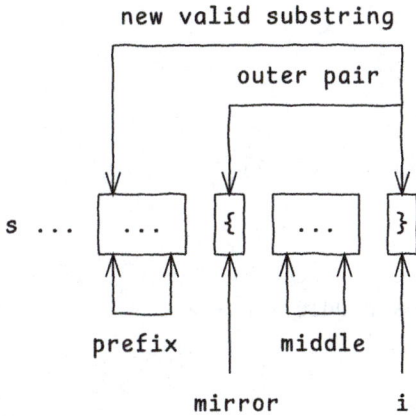

```
                    new valid substring

                          outer pair


  s ...    [  ...  ] [ { ] [  ...  ] [ } ]


           prefix           middle

                    mirror            i
```

This is sufficiently generic to cover more particular cases:

- a simple pair "{}" can be formed with an outer pair having an empty middle;
- prefix may be empty if no valid prefix exists before the outer pair.

If no mirror can be found, or the current character is '{', no valid substring can be formed that ends at the current index.

We keep track of the longest valid substrings found so far in a vector best_ending_at: best_ending_at[i] stores the length of the longest valid substring ending at index i. This allows us to find quickly the mirror index: we just need to skip len(middle) == best_ending_at[i-1] characters.

This algorithm can be implemented as:

```python
def longest_parentheses(s):
    if not s:
        return 0
    # best_ending_at[i] = length of longest valid parentheses
    #                     substring ending at index i.
    best_ending_at = [None] * len(s)
    for i, c in enumerate(s):
        if c == '{' or i == 0:
            # Impossible to form a valid substring ending at i.
            best_ending_at[i] = 0
            continue
        # prefix { middle }   where prefix and middle are valid
        #        ^          ^   and maximal parentheses substrings
        #      mirror       i
        middle_len = best_ending_at[i - 1]
        mirror = i - middle_len - 1
        if mirror < 0 or s[mirror] == '}':
            # Impossible to form a valid substring ending at i:
            # s = ' middle } ... ' or
            # s = ' } middle } ... '
```

```
                best_ending_at[i] = 0
                continue
        if mirror > 0:
            # s = ' prefix { middle } ... '
            prefix_len = best_ending_at[mirror - 1]
        else:
            # s = ' { middle } ... '
            prefix_len = 0
        best_ending_at[i] = prefix_len + middle_len + 2
    # From all valid, maximal substrings, take the longest:
    return max(best_ending_at)
```

The time complexity is $O(n)$, and the space complexity is the same. The space complexity cannot be reduced further, since we need the entire lookup table best_ending_at to find the length of the prefix substring.

Solution 3: dynamic programming, top-down, $O(n)$

We can also write the above algorithm as top-down. We define a helper function get_best_ending_at which computes the length of the longest valid substring ending at a given index. The result of the function needs to be cached to avoid exponential complexity due to redundant calls:

```
from functools import lru_cache


def longest_parentheses(s):
    if not s:
        return 0


    @lru_cache(maxsize=None)
    def get_best_ending_at(i):
        """
        Returns the length of the longest valid parentheses substring
        ending at index i.
        """
        if i == 0 or s[i] == '{':
            # Impossible to form a valid substring ending at i.
            return 0
        # prefix { middle }   where prefix and middle are valid
        #        ^         ^    and maximal parentheses substrings
        #      mirror      i
        middle_len = get_best_ending_at(i - 1)
        mirror = i - middle_len - 1
        if mirror >= 0 and s[mirror] == '{':
            if mirror > 0:
                # s = ' prefix { middle } ... '
```

```
                    prefix_len = get_best_ending_at(mirror - 1)
            else:
                # s = ' { middle } ... '
                prefix_len = 0
            return prefix_len + middle_len + 2
        # Impossible to form a valid substring ending at i.
        return 0

    # From all valid, maximal substrings, take the longest:
    return max(get_best_ending_at(i) for i in range(len(s)))
```

The time and space complexities are both linear.

Unit tests

We first write test cases for very simple strings containing just one pair:

```python
class Testparentheses(unittest.TestCase):
    def test_1_one_pair(self):
        self.assertEqual(longest_parentheses('{}'), 2)
        self.assertEqual(longest_parentheses('{}' + '{'), 2)
        self.assertEqual(longest_parentheses('}' + '{}'), 2)
        self.assertEqual(longest_parentheses('{}' + '}'), 2)
```

We write a test case to make sure we take into account the appending/prepending expansion:

```python
    ...
    def test_2_neighbour_pairs(self):
        self.assertEqual(longest_parentheses('{}{}'), 4)
        self.assertEqual(longest_parentheses('{' + '{}{}'), 4)
        self.assertEqual(longest_parentheses('{}{}' + '{'), 4)
        self.assertEqual(longest_parentheses('{}{}' + '}'), 4)
```

Another test case to cover the nesting expansion:

```python
    ...
    def test_3_nested_pairs(self):
        self.assertEqual(longest_parentheses('{{}}'), 4)
        self.assertEqual(longest_parentheses('{' + '{{}}'), 4)
        self.assertEqual(longest_parentheses('{{}}' + '}'), 4)
        self.assertEqual(longest_parentheses('{{}}' + '{'), 4)
```

Some simple tests to check that we can handle multiple substrings:

```python
    ...
    def test_4_multiple_substrings(self):
        self.assertEqual(longest_parentheses('{}' + '}' + '{{}}' + '{'), 4)
        self.assertEqual(longest_parentheses('{{}}' + '}' + '{}' + '{'), 4)
```

We also cover the edge case where there are no valid substrings:

```
    ...
    def test_5_no_valid_substring(self):
        self.assertEqual(longest_parentheses(''), 0)
        self.assertEqual(longest_parentheses('}'), 0)
        self.assertEqual(longest_parentheses('{'), 0)
        self.assertEqual(longest_parentheses('}}}{{{'), 0)
```

Finally, a test with large input for performance benchmarking:

```
    ...
    def test_6_perf(self):
        n = 1000
        k = 10
        s = ')'.join(['{' * n + '}' * n] * k)
        self.assertEqual(longest_parentheses(s), n * 2)
        s = ')'.join(['{}' * n] * k)
        self.assertEqual(longest_parentheses(s), n * 2)
```

13 Longest increasing subsequence

Given a vector of integers, return the longest subsequence that is monotonically increasing. If there are multiple such subsequences, return any one of them.

Example: For numbers = [1, 4, 2, 1, 5], return [1, 2, 5] or [1, 4, 5].

Clarification questions

Q: How large can the vector be?
A: Up to 1,000 elements.

Q: What answer should be returned when the vector is empty?
A: The empty list.

Solution 1: dynamic programming, bottom-up, $O(n^2)$ time, $O(n^2)$ space

A brute-force solution is to enumerate all monotonically increasing subsequences through backtracking, keeping track of the longest one seen. We do not attempt to implement such a solution, since the complexity is probably exponential.

Instead, let's think about how increasing subsequences could be formed incrementally.

For example, suppose the input vector is numbers = [1, 4, 2, 1, 5]. We can form a one-element subsequence with the first element:

numbers	1	4	2	1	5
subsequences	1				

Let's now look at the second element, 4. We can either form a new subsequence with it, or extend the previous one:

numbers	1	4	2	1	5
subsequences	1				
new subsequences	1	4			
		4			

Let's now look at the third element, 2. We can either form a new subsequence with it, or extend the previous ones where possible:

numbers	1	4	2	1	5
subsequences	1				
		4			
	1	4			
new subsequences			2		
	1		2		

Let's now look at the fourth element, 1. We can only form a new subsequence with it; it is not possible to extend any previous ones since it is smaller or equal to all numbers seen so far:

numbers	1	4	2	1	5
subsequences	1				
		4			
	1	4			
			2		
	1		2		
new subsequences				1	

Let's now look at the fifth element, 5. We can form a new subsequence with it, or extend previous ones:

numbers	1	4	2	1	5
subsequences	1				
		4			
	1	4			
			2		
	1		2		
				1	
new subsequences					5
	1				5
		4			5
	1	4			5
			2		5
	1		2		5
				1	5

Among all the subsequences we computed, there are both of the longest increasing subsequences ([1, 2, 5] and [1, 4, 5]). However, we have also computed a lot of smaller subsequences that are not useful.

For example, there is no point in storing subsequence [4] when we know that there is a longer subsequence ending with 4: [1, 4]. They both have the same potential for future expansion, but the latter is longer, so preferrable.

Let's look at the steps of the procedure again, with such redundant sequences removed:

numbers	1	4	2	1	5	
subsequences	1					step 1: subsequences ending with 1
	1	4				step 2: subsequences ending with 4
	1		2			step 3: subsequences ending with 2
				1		step 4: subsequences ending with 1
	1	4			5	step 5: subsequences ending with 5
	1		2		5	(same length: we can store either one)

To summarize:

If there are n elements in the vector, there are n steps. In step i, we consider subsequences ending with numbers[i]. We have the following options:

- A subsequence consisting only of numbers[i];
- Extending previous subsequences with numbers[i].

We choose the longest one, and continue to the next step.

The overall longest increasing subsequence is the longest one seen.

We can implement this algorithm as:

```python
def longest_increasing_subsequence(numbers):
    # Handle empty case straight away.
    if not numbers:
        return []
    # longest_ending_at[i] = longest sequence ending with numbers[i].
    longest_ending_at = []
    for number in numbers:
        # Longest sequence ending with `number`.
        # Initially we form just `[number]`.
        best_seq = [number]
        # Consider all the sequences found so far.
        for seq in longest_ending_at:
            # Can we extend it monotonically with `number`?
            if seq[-1] < number:
                # Does it lead to a longer sequence?
                if len(seq) + 1 > len(best_seq):
                    best_seq = seq + [number]
```

```
        # Store the result.
        longest_ending_at.append(best_seq)
    # Return the longest sequence.
    return max(longest_ending_at, key=len)
```

The time complexity of the algorithm is $O(n^2)$ and the space complexity is $O(n^2)$ as well, since we store n partial sequences of length up to n.

Solution 2: dynamic programming, bottom-up, $O(n^2)$ time, $O(n)$ space

We can optimize the problem by reducing space complexity, using linked lists to store the subsequences in a compressed form.

Here is an approach that encodes the linked lists backwards using an array: Suppose that parent_longest_ending_at[i] stores the predecessor of numbers[i] in the sequence, or -1 if there is no predecessor.

For example, [1, 4, 5] can be stored as:

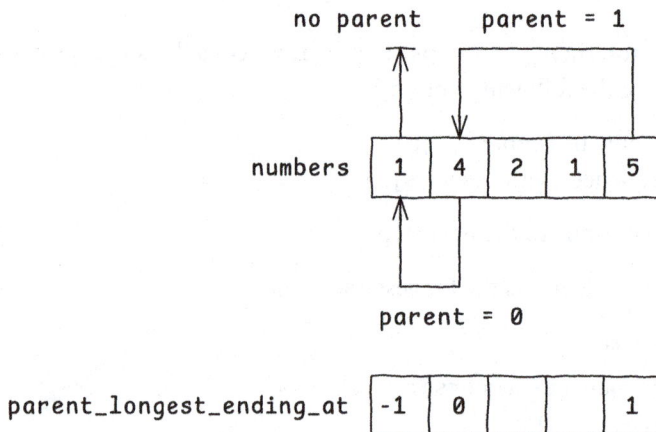

To reconstruct a sequence, we have to walk over the parent pointers in reverse.

Here is an optimized implementation:

```
def longest_increasing_subsequence(numbers):
    # Handle empty case straight away.
    if not numbers:
        return []


    # len_longest_ending_at[i] = length of the longest sequence ending
    #                            with numbers[i].
    len_longest_ending_at = []
    # Store sequences efficiently:
    # parent_longest_ending_at[i] = index of previous element in the
    #       longest sequence ending with numbers[i],
```

```
#           or -1 if numbers[i] is the first element in the sequence.
parent_longest_ending_at = []
for number in numbers:
    # Length of the longest sequence ending with `number`.
    # Initially we form just `[number]`, so the length is 1.
    best_len = 1
    # Parent of `number` in the sequence. Initially there is no parent.
    best_parent = -1
    # Consider all the sequences found so far ending at i
    # (some element on the left of `number`).
    for i, seq_len in enumerate(len_longest_ending_at):
        # Can we extend it monotonically with `number`?
        if numbers[i] < number:
            # Does it lead to a longer sequence?
            if best_len < seq_len + 1:
                best_len = seq_len + 1
                best_parent = i
    # Store the result.
    len_longest_ending_at.append(best_len)
    parent_longest_ending_at.append(best_parent)

# Return the sequence ending with `numbers[i]`,
# using `parent_longest_ending_at` to reconstruct it.
def reconstruct(i):
    if parent_longest_ending_at[i] != -1:
        # Reconstruct the prefix.
        prefix = reconstruct(parent_longest_ending_at[i])
    else:
        # We reached the first item, there is no prefix.
        prefix = []
    # Append the current item.
    prefix.append(numbers[i])
    return prefix

# Reconstruct the longest sequence.
best_len_overall = max(len_longest_ending_at)
for i, seq_len in enumerate(len_longest_ending_at):
    if seq_len == best_len_overall:
        return reconstruct(i)
```

The time complexity of the algorithm is $O(n^2)$ and the space complexity is now reduced to $O(n)$.

Variant: count the number of solutions

Given a vector of integers, return the *number* of longest subsequences that are monotonically increasing.

Example: For numbers = [1, 4, 2, 1, 5], since there are two possible longest subsequences: [1, 2, 5] and [1, 4, 5], return 2.

Solution: dynamic programming, bottom-up, $O(n^2)$ time, $O(n)$ space

We adapt the solution that finds the longest subsequence to compute for each element:

- The length of the longest subsequence ending with the element;
- The number of longest subsequence ending with the element.

We initialize the longest subsequence ending with the element with [element], such that it has length of 1 and count of 1.

For example, this is the initial subsequence we would form for element 4:

```
subsequences   | 4                    |    ending with 4: count = 1
```

When we find a longer previous subsequence that can be extended with the current element, we change the length and propagate the previous counter.

For example, if there are 3 subsequences ending with 2, and the current element is 4, we can form as well 3 subsequences ending with 4 by extending the previous ones:

```
subsequences   | 1   2         |
               | 0   2         |    ending with 2: count = 3
               | -1  2         |
               |               |
               | 1   2   4     |
               | 0   2   4     |    ending with 4: count = 3
               | -1  2   4     |
```

When we find a tie (another previous subsequence that can be extended with the current number to form a subsequence of length equal to the longest so far), we need to sum up the two counters:

```
subsequences    1   2
                0   2          ending with 2: count = 3
               -1   2

                2   3          ending with 3: count = 2
                0   3

                1   2   4
                0   2   4
               -1   2   4      ending with 4: count = 2 + 3 = 5
                2   3   4
                0   3   4
```

We can implement the algorithm as:

```python
def count_longest_increasing_subsequences(numbers):
    # Handle empty case straight away.
    if not numbers:
        return 0
    # len_longest_ending_at[i] = length of the longest sequence ending
    #                            with numbers[i].
    len_longest_ending_at = []
    # count_longest_ending_at[i] = number of longest sequences ending
    #                              with numbers[i].
    count_longest_ending_at = []
    for number in numbers:
        # Length of the longest sequence ending with `number`.
        # Initially we form just `[number]`, so the length is 1.
        best_len = 1
        # Number of longest sequences ending with `number`.
        # Initially there is just one.
        best_count = 1
        # Consider all the sequences found so far ending at i
        # (some element on the left of `number`).
        for i, seq_len in enumerate(len_longest_ending_at):
            # Can we extend it monotonically with `number`?
            if numbers[i] < number:
                # Does it lead to a longer sequence?
                if best_len < seq_len + 1:
                    best_len = seq_len + 1
                    best_count = count_longest_ending_at[j]
                # Is it a tie?
                elif best_len == seq_len + 1:
                    best_count += count_longest_ending_at[j]
        len_longest_ending_at.append(best_len)
        count_longest_ending_at.append(best_count)
```

```
# Length of the longest sequence.
best_len_overall = max(len_longest_ending_at)
# Sum up all the counters for sequences of optimal length.
return sum([count for i, count in enumerate(count_longest_ending_at)
            if len_longest_ending_at[i] == best_len_overall])
```

The time complexity is $O(n^2)$ and the space complexity is $O(n)$.

14 Longest arithmetic subsequence

Given a vector of integers numbers, return the length of the longest arithmetic subsequence.

A sequence is called arithmetic if the difference between any two consecutive numbers is the same, for example: [2, 4, 6, 8, 10].

Example: For numbers = [1, 2, 3, 5, 8, 7], return 4, which is the length of the subsequence [1, 3, 5, 7].

Clarification questions

Q: How large can the vector be?
A: Up to 1,000 elements.

Q: What answer should be returned when the vector is empty?
A: Zero.

Q: What answer should be returned when the vector contains a single element?
A: One.

Q: Should we consider subsequences that are decreasing? Such as [5, 3, 1].
A: Yes, those are valid arithmetic subsequences.

Q: Should we consider subsequences that are constant? Such as [1, 1, 1].
A: Yes, those are valid arithmetic subsequences as well.

Solution 1: dynamic programming, bottom-up, $O(n^2)$ time, $O(n^2)$ space

We suspect that this problem can be solved with dynamic programming, since it is similar to the longest increasing subsequence problem. We try to find a similar solution, based on forming subsequences incrementally.

Consider the example numbers = [1, 2, 3, 5, 8, 7]. For the first number, we can form a one-element subsequence:

numbers	1	2	3	5	8	7
subsequences	1					

Let's now look at the second element, 2. We can either form a new subsequence with it, or extend the previous one. If we extend, we obtain a sequence of length 2, so we can already compute the step of the sequence (the difference between consecutive elements):

numbers	1	2	3	5	8	7	
subsequences	1						step = ?
		2					step = ?
	1	2					step = 1

Let's now look at the third element, 3. We can either form a new subsequence with it, or extend the previous ones where the step matches:

numbers	1	2	3	5	8	7	
subsequences	1						step = ?
		2					step = ?
	1	2					step = 1
			3				step = ?
		2	3				step = 1
	1		3				step = 2
	1	2	3				step = 1

Notice that we have multiple subsequences with step 1 ending at 3: [2, 3] and [1, 2, 3]. Let's keep just the longest one, since the shorter one cannot be part of the final solution:

numbers	1	2	3	5	8	7	
subsequences	1						step = ?
		2					step = ?
	1	2					step = 1
			3				step = ?
	1		3				step = 2
	1	2	3				step = 1

Let's now look at element 5. We can either form a new subsequence with it, or extend previous one where possible:

numbers	1	2	3	5	8	7	
subsequences	1						step = ?
		2					step = ?
	1	2					step = 1
			3				step = ?
	1		3				step = 2
	1	2	3				step = 1
				5			step = ?
	1			5			step = 4
		2		5			step = 3
	1		3	5			step = 2

Note that we could not extend the one ending at 3 with step 1, since the difference between 3 and 5 is 2, so the step does not match.

Let's now look at element 8. Here we can form only subsequences of two elements:

numbers	1	2	3	5	8	7	
subsequences	1						step = ?
		2					step = ?
	1	2					step = 1
			3				step = ?
	1		3				step = 2
	1	2	3				step = 1
				5			step = ?
	1			5			step = 4
		2		5			step = 3
	1		3	5			step = 2
					8		step = ?
	1				8		step = 7
		2			8		step = 6
			3		8		step = 5
				5	8		step = 3

Finally, we look at element 7. Here we find a new global maximum, extending the subsequence of step 2 ending at 5, [1, 3, 5]:

numbers	1	2	3	5	8	7	
subsequences	1						step = ?
		2					step = ?
	1	2					step = 1
			3				step = ?
	1		3				step = 2
	1	2	3				step = 1
				5			step = ?
	1			5			step = 4
		2		5			step = 3
	1		3	5			step = 2
					8		step = ?
	1				8		step = 7
		2			8		step = 6
			3		8		step = 5
				5	8		step = 3
						7	step = ?
	1					7	step = 6
		2				7	step = 5
			3			7	step = 4
	1		3	5		7	step = 2
					8	7	step = -1

Based on the example, we propose the following procedure to find the longest arithmetic subsequence:

- Iterate over the vector from left to right. For each element in the vector, consider each element on its left:
  - Compute the step as the difference between the current element and the element on the left.
  - If a subsequence with that step exists ending at the element on the left, extend it with the current element. Store only the length of the longest subsequence of each step value.

We return the longest subsequence seen overall. We also need to be careful to handle the edge cases where there is just one element, or where there are no elements.

We can implement the solution as:

```
def longest_arithmetic_subsequence(numbers):
    # Handle the edge cases where there are less than 2 elements.
    # The rest of the code assumes that there are at least 2 elements,
    # so that we do not have undefined arithmetic subsequence steps.
    if not numbers:
```

```
        return 0
    if len(numbers) == 1:
        return 1
    # best_length[i][step] = length of the longest arithmetic subsequence
    #      having step `step` and ending with the i-th number.
    best_length = [{} for _ in numbers]
    # Length of the longest arithmetic subsequence found overall.
    best_length_global = 0
    for i, number in enumerate(numbers):
        # We try to extend previous subsequences.
        # For each number on the left, we can form or continue a different
        # subsequence:
        for left in range(i):
            step = number - numbers[left]
            # Option 1: start a new subsequence from the pair of numbers.
            new_sequence_length = 2
            # Option 2: extend the previous subsequence, if one exists.
            continuing_sequence_length = 1 + best_length[left].get(step, 0)
            # We always choose the longest subsequence.
            best_length[i][step] = max(new_sequence_length,
                                        continuing_sequence_length)
            # Update global result.
            best_length_global = max(best_length_global,
                                      best_length[i][step])
    return best_length_global
```

The time complexity is clearly $O(n^2)$ due to the two nested loops. The space complexity is $O(n^2)$, since we create a dictionary with up to n values for each number.

Unit tests

We propose three unit tests:

- A test to cover simple cases, where the result can be easily checked by hand.
- A test to cover edge cases:
    - The empty vector.
    - A vector with just one element.
    - A vector that is an arithmetic sequence.
- A test to check performance with large inputs, at the upper limit of the requirements.

```
class Test(unittest.TestCase):
    def test_1_simple(self):
        self.assertEqual(longest_arithmetic_subsequence(range(5)), 5)
        self.assertEqual(longest_arithmetic_subsequence(
                [1, 2, 3, 5, 8, 7]), 4)
```

```python
def test_2_edge_case(self):
    self.assertEqual(longest_arithmetic_subsequence([1]), 1)
    self.assertEqual(longest_arithmetic_subsequence([1, 2]), 2)
    self.assertEqual(longest_arithmetic_subsequence(
            list(range(10))), 10)
    self.assertEqual(longest_arithmetic_subsequence(
            list(range(10)[::-1])), 10)

def test_3_perf(self):
    n = 500
    fwd = list(range(n))
    rev = fwd[::-1]
    numbers = [x for tuple in zip(fwd, rev) for x in tuple]
    self.assertEqual(longest_arithmetic_subsequence(numbers), n)
```

15 Dealing the best hand of cards

Given a deck of cards, we have to deal a hand containing a certain number of cards. Cards can be dealt from the top of the deck as well as from the bottom. Determine the best hand that can be dealt, in terms of the sum of the values of the cards, assuming each card has a specific value.

Example: for the deck [3, 1, 1, 6, 2], we can deal the following hands of 3 cards: [3, 1, 1], [3, 1, 2], [3, 2, 6], [2, 6, 1]. The best hand is [3, 2, 6] with sum 11.

Clarification questions

Q: Does the dealer know the values of the cards in the deck and their order?
A: Yes, assume complete knowledge of the deck.

Q: How large can a hand be?
A: The size limit is 1,000,000 cards.

Q: Can the hand be empty?
A: Yes. In that case, its value is 0.

Q: What if there are not enough cards in the deck to build a hand of the requested size?
A: Then the whole deck should be dealt.

We asked the clarification questions to learn how to handle the edge cases, as well as find out what are the time complexity constraints for the solution. To handle 1 million cards, we must look for an algorithm with time complexity around $O(n)$ or $O(n \log n)$.

Solution 1: brute force, $O(n^2)$ time

A straightforward solution is to enumerate all possible hands and choose the best one. Suppose the hand size is n. We can deal the following hands:

- all n cards from the bottom;
- n - 1 cards from the bottom and 1 from the top;
- n - 2 cards from the bottom and 2 from the top;
- ...
- all n cards from the top.

This can be also seen in the following figure:

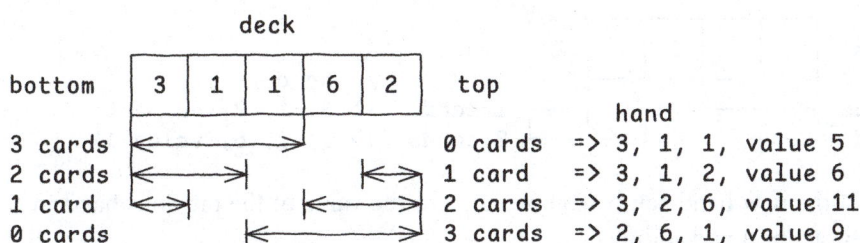

```
                    deck
bottom      ┌───┬───┬───┬───┬───┐
            │ 3 │ 1 │ 1 │ 6 │ 2 │   top
            └───┴───┴───┴───┴───┘
                                              hand
3 cards  ←──────────────→        0 cards  => 3, 1, 1, value 5
2 cards  ←────────→        ←───→  1 card   => 3, 1, 2, value 6
1 card   ←→         ←──────────→  2 cards  => 3, 2, 6, value 11
0 cards             ←──────────────→  3 cards  => 2, 6, 1, value 9
```

This method can be implemented as:

```
def get_best_hand_from_deck(deck, hand_size):
    # Handle the case where the deck is too small.
    if hand_size >= len(deck):
        return sum(deck)
    # Keep track of the best known hand.
    best_hand = 0
    for num_top in range(hand_size + 1):
        num_bottom = hand_size - num_top
        # Deal num_bottom cards from the bottom...
        bottom = sum(deck[0:num_bottom])
        # and num_top cards from the top.
        top = sum(deck[-num_top:]) if num_top else 0
        hand = bottom + top
        # Update the best hand if needed.
        best_hand = max(best_hand, hand)
    return best_hand
```

The above code is correct but too slow: for a hand of size n, it performs n iterations, and in each one performs n steps to compute the value of the hand. The overall time complexity is $O(n^2)$.

Solution 2: dynamic programming, $O(n)$ time

We can optimize the previous solution by noticing that we can avoid redundant summation when computing the values of the hands, by reusing the sums that have already been computed.

For example, consider the following hand:

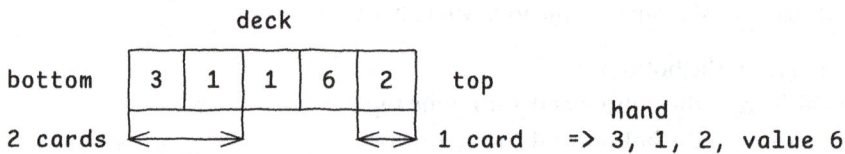

```
                      deck
bottom    | 3 | 1 | 1 | 6 | 2 |  top
                                         hand
2 cards   <--------->    <--->  1 card  => 3, 1, 2, value 6
```

The next hand in the iteration differs from the current one in just 2 cards: the 1 to be removed and the 6 to be added:

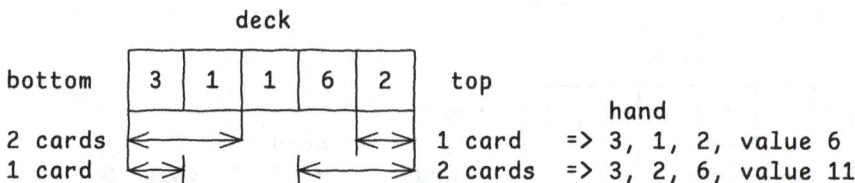

```
                      deck
bottom    | 3 | 1 | 1 | 6 | 2 |  top
                                         hand
2 cards   <--------->    <--->  1 card  => 3, 1, 2, value 6
1 card    <-->      <--------->  2 cards => 3, 2, 6, value 11
```

The value of the new hand can be computed from the value of the previous hand in $O(1)$ steps by subtracting 1 and adding 6.

Based on this reasoning, we can rewrite the algorithm as:

```
def get_best_hand_from_deck(deck, hand_size):
    # Handle the case where the deck is too small.
    if hand_size >= len(deck):
        return sum(deck)
    # Start with a hand dealing only from the bottom of the deck.
    num_top = 0
    num_bottom = hand_size
    hand = sum(deck[0:num_bottom])
    # Keep track of the best known hand.
    best_hand = hand
    while num_top < hand_size:
        # Give up the deepest card from the bottom,
        # replacing it with a card dealt from the top.
        num_bottom -= 1
        num_top += 1
        hand -= deck[num_bottom]
        hand += deck[-num_top]
        # Update the best hand if needed.
        best_hand = max(best_hand, hand)
    return best_hand
```

This has $O(n)$ time complexity in terms of the hand size n.

Unit tests

For testing, we first cover simple, normal cases to make sure the algorithm works at all and to ease potential troubleshooting.

Then we cover edge cases, such as:

- the empty deck;
- a hand size covering the whole deck;
- a hand size larger than the deck.

Finally, we write a performance test using a large input, to ensure the implementation is fast enough given the requirements, as well as to catch possible future performance regressions.

The unit tests can be written as:

```
class TestBestHand(unittest.TestCase):
    def test_1_simple(self):
        self.assertEqual(get_best_hand_from_deck([2, 2, 1, 4, 1], 2), 5)
        self.assertEqual(get_best_hand_from_deck([2, 1, 1, 4, 1], 3), 7)

    def test_2_empty_hand(self):
        self.assertEqual(get_best_hand_from_deck([2, 2, 1, 4, 1], 0), 0)

    def test_3_whole_deck(self):
```

```
        self.assertEqual(get_best_hand_from_deck([2, 2, 1, 4, 1], 5), 10)

    def test_4_perf(self):
        n = 200000
        deck = [3] * n + [2] * n + [1] * n + [5] * n + [4] * n
        self.assertEqual(get_best_hand_from_deck(deck, 3 * n),
                         (5 + 4 + 3) * n)
```

16 Number of ways to climb stairs

Count the number of ways to climb a staircase with n steps, if you are allowed to climb either one step or two steps at a time.

Example: For n = 2, there are 2 ways to climb the stairs:

- climb one step, then another step;
- climb two steps at a time directly to the second step.

Clarification questions

Q: How large can n be?
A: Up to 50.

Q: Can n be zero or negative? How should invalid values be handled?
A: n >= 1. You may assume that no invalid values are passed.

Solution 1: dynamic programming, top-down, $O(n)$ time

For any step i >= 2, we can reach it in only two ways:

- climbing a step from step i-1;
- climbing two steps at a time from step i-2.

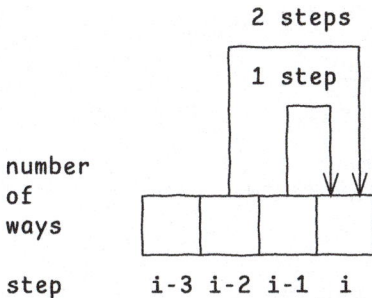

The total number of ways we can reach step i is thus the sum of the number of ways we can reach step i-1 and the number of ways we can reach step i-2.

We can implement this function recursively. We just need to handle the termination condition: i <= 1. In these cases, the number of ways we can get there is 1:

- climbing to the first step can be done in just one way;
- climbing to the "zero" step means just standing on the starting position, which also can be achieved in one way.

We can now implement the function recursively with caching:

```
from functools import lru_cache


@lru_cache(maxsize=None)
def count_num_paths_stairs(n):
```

```
    if n <= 1:
        return 1
    num_paths_one_step = count_num_paths_stairs(n - 1)
    num_paths_two_steps = count_num_paths_stairs(n - 2)
    return num_paths_one_step + num_paths_two_steps
```

This solution has $O(n)$ time complexity and $O(n)$ space complexity.

Interestingly, this recursion matches exactly the formula for computing the Fibonacci sequence.

Solution 2: dynamic programming, bottom-up, $O(n)$ time

We can apply the same reasoning when starting from lower step counts and advancing to higher step counts, to find an iterative solution:

```
def count_num_paths_stairs(n):
    if n <= 1:
        return 1
    # num_paths[i] = number of paths to climb to i-th step.
    num_paths = [0] * (n + 1)
    # Initial position: just one possible way to get there.
    num_paths[0] = 1
    # First step: just one possible way to get there.
    num_paths[1] = 1
    for i in range(2, n + 1):
        num_paths_one_step = num_paths[i - 1]
        num_paths_two_steps = num_paths[i - 2]
        num_paths[i] = num_paths_one_step + num_paths_two_steps
    return num_paths[n]
```

This solution has $O(n)$ time complexity and $O(n)$ space complexity.

Solution 3: dynamic programming, bottom-up, $O(1)$ time

The iterative solution does not require storing the entire vector num_paths, just the last two elements. We can rewrite it in a way that is more memory-efficient:

```
def count_num_paths_stairs(n):
    if n <= 1:
        return 1
    # Initial position: just one possible way to get there.
    num_paths_prev = 1
    # First step: just one possible way to get there.
    num_paths_current = 1
    for i in range(2, n + 1):
        num_paths_one_step = num_paths_current
```

```
        num_paths_two_steps = num_paths_prev
        num_paths_prev = num_paths_current
        num_paths_current = num_paths_one_step + num_paths_two_steps
    return num_paths_current
```

This solution has $O(n)$ time complexity and $O(1)$ space complexity.

Unit tests

For testing, we first cover simple cases to make sure the algorithm works and can be debugged easily:

```
class TestStairs(unittest.TestCase):
    def test_1_simple(self):
        self.assertEqual(count_num_paths_stairs(2), 2)
        self.assertEqual(count_num_paths_stairs(4), 5)
```

Then we address edge cases:

```
    ...
    def test_2_edge_cases(self):
        self.assertEqual(count_num_paths_stairs(1), 1)
```

Finally, we write a test for large values of n to ensure that the performance is satisfactory:

```
    ...
    def test_3_perf(self):
        self.assertEqual(count_num_paths_stairs(35), 14930352)
        self.assertEqual(count_num_paths_stairs(49), 12586269025)
```

17 Number of paths through maze

You are given a maze represented as a matrix, where cells you may enter are marked with zeroes, and walls are marked with ones. You start at the top-left corner, and need to reach the bottom-right corner. You are only allowed to move to the right or down, without passing through walls. Count how many distinct paths exist.

Example:

```
maze = [
    [0, 0, 1],
    [0, 0, 0],
]
```

There are two possible paths from the top-left corner to the bottom-right corner:

Clarification questions

Q: How large can the maze be?
A: Up to 50 rows and columns.

Q: Can there be walls in the starting or ending positions?
A: Yes. In that case the number of paths is zero.

Q: Can cells contain values other than 0 or 1?
A: No.

Solution 1: dynamic programming, top-down, $O(n^2)$ time

Consider an arbitrary cell (row, col). We can reach it in only two ways:

- coming from above, unless there is a wall above or the cell is on the top row;
- coming from the left, unless there is a wall to the left or the cell is on the first column.

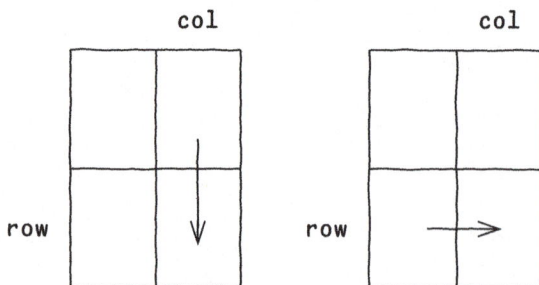

Suppose that there are 7 paths from the top-left corner to the cell above, and 8 paths from the top-left corner to the cell on the left. Then the number of distinct paths from the top-left corner to the cell is 7 + 8 = 15. This is because we can take each of the 7 paths reaching the cell above and extend it by adding a step down; and similarly we can extend each of the 8 paths reaching the cell on the left, to form a total of 15 distinct paths that reach our cell:

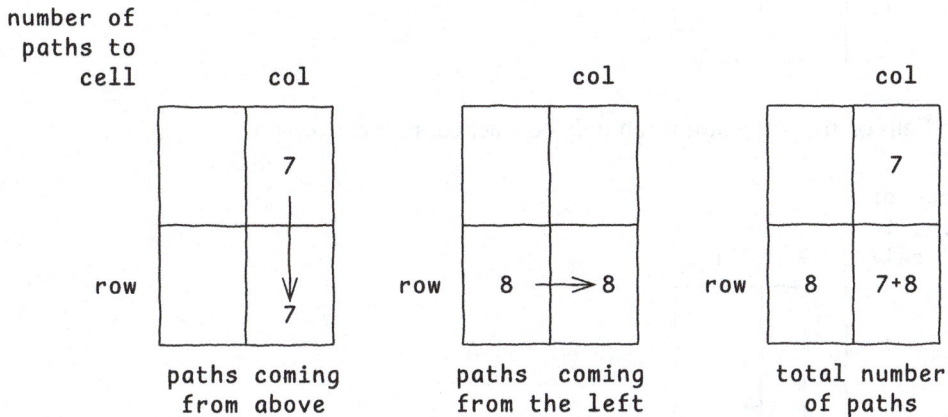

```
number of
paths to
   cell          col                      col                       col
           ┌─────┬─────┐            ┌─────┬─────┐            ┌─────┬─────┐
           │     │  7  │            │     │     │            │     │  7  │
           │     │  │  │            │     │     │            │     │     │
           ├─────┼──┼──┤            ├─────┼─────┤            ├─────┼─────┤
    row    │     │  ▼  │     row    │  8 ─┼─▶ 8 │     row    │  8  │ 7+8 │
           │     │  7  │            │     │     │            │     │     │
           └─────┴─────┘            └─────┴─────┘            └─────┴─────┘
           paths coming             paths  coming            total number
           from above               from the left             of paths
```

Based on this logic, we can implement a function that computes the count using recursion. We just need to handle the special cases:

- The top-left corner is the starting position, so it can be reached in just one way:

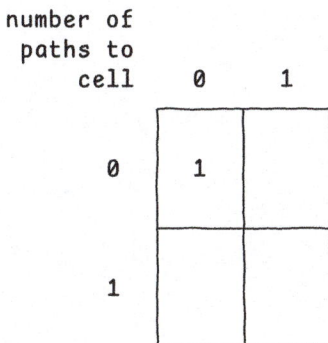

```
number of
paths to
   cell     0     1
         ┌─────┬─────┐
     0   │  1  │     │
         │     │     │
         ├─────┼─────┤
     1   │     │     │
         │     │     │
         └─────┴─────┘
```

- Cells on the first row can only be reached from the left:

```
number of
 paths to
    cell    i       i+1
```

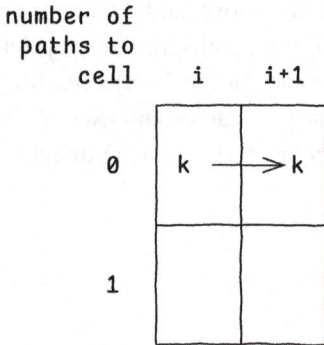

- Cells on the first column can only be reached from above:

```
number of
 paths to
    cell    0       1
```

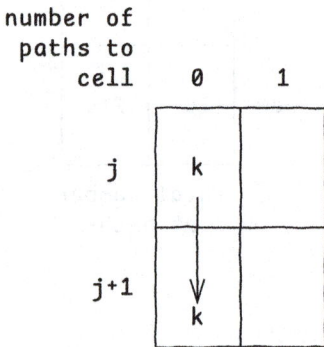

- Cells that contain a wall cannot be reached:

```
number of
 paths to
    cell    i       i+1
```

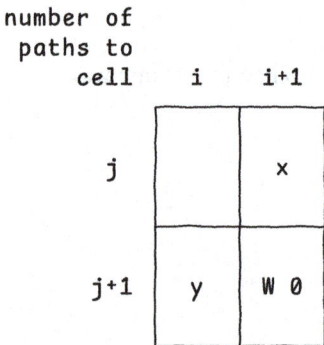

We can now implement the function recursively with caching:

```python
from functools import lru_cache


def count_num_paths(maze):
    WALL = 1
    @lru_cache(maxsize=None)
    def count_num_paths_to_cell(row, col):
        # Invalid cell: no paths
```

```
        if row < 0 or col < 0 or maze[row][col] == WALL:
            return 0
        # Starting position: 1 option
        if row == 0 and col == 0:
            return 1
        # Sum up the number of paths incoming from all
        # possible directions:
        num_from_above = count_num_paths_to_cell(row - 1, col)
        num_from_left = count_num_paths_to_cell(row, col - 1)
        return num_from_above + num_from_left
    num_rows = len(maze)
    num_cols = len(maze[0])
    # Return the number of paths reaching the bottom-right cell.
    return count_num_paths_to_cell(num_rows - 1, num_cols - 1)
```

This solution has $O(n^2)$ time complexity and $O(n^2)$ space complexity, since the helper function count_num_paths_to_cell may be called at most once per cell.

Solution 2: dynamic programming, bottom-up, $O(n^2)$ time

We can apply the same reasoning but in the opposite order:

- We start from the top-left corner, where we can have just 1 path;
- We propagate the number of paths reaching the current cell to the right and below;
- We set the number of paths to zero in cells that contain a wall;
- We iterate over cells in an order where the cell above and the cell on the left of the current cell have already had their paths counted.

```
def count_num_paths(maze):
    WALL = 1
    num_rows = len(maze)
    num_cols = len(maze[0])
    # num_paths_to_cell[row][col] = number of paths that can reach
    #                               cell (row, col). Initially 0.
    num_paths_to_cell = [[0] * num_cols for _ in range(num_rows)]
    for row in range(num_rows):
        for col in range(num_cols):
            if maze[row][col] == WALL:
                # No paths can pass through this cell.
                num_paths_to_cell[row][col] = 0
            elif row == 0 and col == 0:
                # Starting position: just 1 path.
                num_paths_to_cell[row][col] = 1
            else:
                if row > 0:
                    num_from_above = num_paths_to_cell[row - 1][col]
```

```
        else:
            # Top row: nothing above.
            num_from_above = 0
        if col > 0:
            num_from_left = num_paths_to_cell[row][col - 1]
        else:
            # First column: nothing on the left.
            num_from_left = 0
        num_paths_to_cell[row][col] = (num_from_above +
                                            num_from_left)
    # Return the number of paths reaching the bottom-right cell.
    return num_paths_to_cell[-1][-1]
```

This solution has $O(n^2)$ time complexity and $O(n^2)$ space complexity, since we are iterating over the entire matrix and storing the path count of each cell.

Solution 3: dynamic programming, bottom-up, $O(n^2)$ time, linear space

The iterative solution does not require storing the entire matrix num_paths_to_cell, just the last row and the next one to be computed. We can rewrite it in a way that is more memory-efficient:

```
def count_num_paths3(maze):
    WALL = 1
    num_rows = len(maze)
    num_cols = len(maze[0])
    # npaths_prev_row[col] = number of paths that can reach the cells
    #                        from the previous row.
    npaths_prev_row = [0] * num_cols
    # npaths_next_row[col] = number of paths that can reach the cells
    #                        from the current row.
    npaths_next_row = [0] * num_cols
    for row in range(num_rows):
        # Use npaths_prev_row to compute npaths_next_row.
        for col in range(num_cols):
            if maze[row][col] == WALL:
                # No paths can pass through this cell.
                npaths_next_row[col] = 0
            elif row == 0 and col == 0:
                # Starting position: just 1 path.
                npaths_next_row[col] = 1
            else:
                if row > 0:
                    num_from_above = npaths_prev_row[col]
                else:
                    # Top row: nothing above.
```

```
                num_from_above = 0
            if col > 0:
                num_from_left = npaths_next_row[col - 1]
            else:
                # First column: nothing on the left.
                num_from_left = 0
            npaths_next_row[col] = num_from_above + num_from_left
        # Swap buffers.
        npaths_prev_row, npaths_next_row = npaths_next_row, npaths_prev_row
    # Return the number of paths reaching the bottom-right cell.
    return npaths_prev_row[-1]
```

This solution has $O(n^2)$ time complexity and $O(n)$ space complexity.

Unit tests

For testing, we first cover simple cases without walls:

```
class TestMaze(unittest.TestCase):
    def test_1_no_walls(self):
        maze = [
            [0, 0],
            [0, 0],
        ]
        self.assertEqual(count_num_paths(maze), 2)
        maze = [
            [0, 0, 0],
            [0, 0, 0],
        ]
        self.assertEqual(count_num_paths(maze), 3)
        maze = [
            [0, 0],
            [0, 0],
            [0, 0],
        ]
        self.assertEqual(count_num_paths(maze), 3)
```

Then we cover some simple cases with walls:

```
    ...
    def test_2_walls(self):
        maze = [
            [0, 1],
            [0, 0],
        ]
        self.assertEqual(count_num_paths(maze), 1)
        maze = [
```

```
            [0, 1, 0],
            [0, 0, 0],
        ]
        self.assertEqual(count_num_paths(maze), 1)
        maze = [
            [0, 0],
            [1, 0],
            [0, 0],
        ]
        self.assertEqual(count_num_paths(maze), 1)
        maze = [
            [0, 0, 1],
            [0, 0, 0],
        ]
        self.assertEqual(count_num_paths(maze), 2)
```

We also cover some edge cases: a maze with just one cell, and a maze without any paths to the destination:

```
    ...
    def test_3_one_cell_maze(self):
        maze = [
            [0],
        ]
        self.assertEqual(count_num_paths(maze), 1)

    def test_4_no_paths(self):
        maze = [
            [1],
        ]
        self.assertEqual(count_num_paths(maze), 0)
        maze = [
            [0, 1],
            [1, 0],
        ]
        self.assertEqual(count_num_paths(maze), 0)
```

Finally, we write a test for large values of n to ensure that the performance is satisfactory:

```
    ...
    def test_5_perf(self):
        n = 50
        maze = [
            [0] * n,
        ] * n
        # No walls: all paths have length N = 2 * n - 2 steps,
        # out of which K = n - 1 are down.
```

```
# There are (N choose K) distinct choices.
self.assertEqual(count_num_paths(maze), math.comb(2*n - 2, n - 1))
```

Counting problems

We have seen a series of problems that involved counting; unlike previous problems that involved some form of optimization. Both are common applications of dynamic programming.

18   Maximum-score path through maze

You are given a maze represented as a matrix. Cells that you cannot enter are marked with -1; the rest of the cells contain a non-negative integer that represents a score. The score of a path through the maze is equal to the sum of the scores of the cells traversed by that path.

You start at the top-left corner, and need to reach the bottom-right corner, making moves only to the right or down.

Return the best possible score you can obtain.

Example:

```
maze = [
    [1, 2, -1],
    [1, 3,  0],
]
```

There are two possible paths from the top-left corner to the bottom-right corner, the best one having score 6:

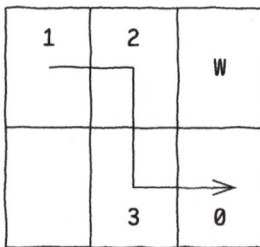   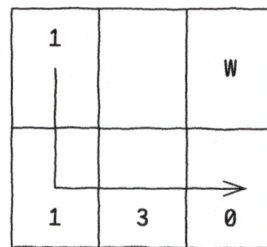

```
score: 1 + 2 + 3 + 0 = 6        1 + 1 + 3 + 0 = 5
```

Clarification questions

Q: How large can the maze be?
A: Up to 50 rows and columns.

Q: Is it possible that no path to the destination exists?
A: Yes. In that case, return -1.

Q: Can there be walls in the starting or ending positions?
A: Yes. In that case, return -1.

Solution 1: dynamic programming, top-down, $O(n^2)$ time

We can use a similar approach as to the problem of counting the number of possible paths through the maze.

Consider an arbitrary cell (`row`, `col`) with cell score `x` `>=` `0`. We can reach it in only two ways:

- coming from above, unless there is a wall above or the cell is on the top row;
- coming from the left, unless there is a wall to the left or the cell is on the first column.

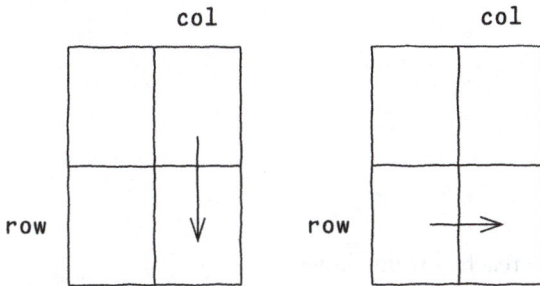

Suppose that the score of the best path reaching the cell above is 3, and the score of the best path reaching the cell to the left is 4. Then the best option to reach the current cell is extending the path from the left:

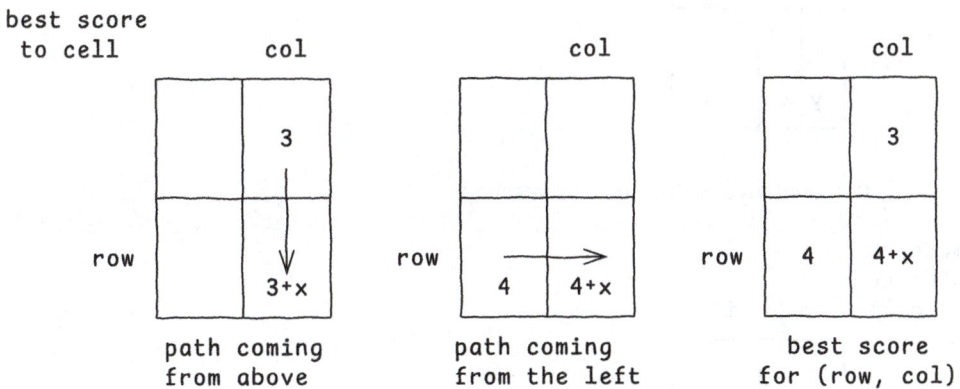

We can implement this function recursively. We just need to handle the special cases:

- The top-left corner is the starting position, so the path's score is the cell's score:

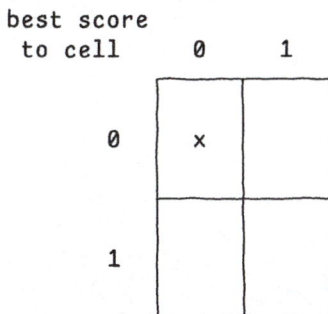

- Cells on the first row can only be reached from the left:

```
best score
  to cell      i     i+1
```

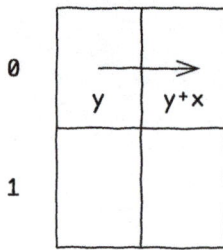

- Cells on the first column can only be reached from above:

```
best score
  to cell      0      1
```

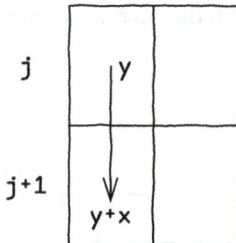

- Cells that contain a wall cannot be reached:

```
number of
 paths to
    cell      i     i+1
```

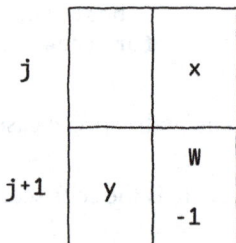

We can implement this function recursively with caching:

```python
from functools import lru_cache


def find_best_path(maze):
    WALL = -1
    IMPOSSIBLE = -1
    @lru_cache(maxsize=None)
    def find_best_score_to_cell(row, col):
        # Invalid cell: no paths
        if row < 0 or col < 0 or maze[row][col] == WALL:
```

```
            return IMPOSSIBLE
        # Starting position: score of the first cell.
        if row == 0 and col == 0:
            return maze[row][col]
        # Find the best paths incoming from all
        # possible directions:
        best_from_above = find_best_score_to_cell(row - 1, col)
        best_from_left = find_best_score_to_cell(row, col - 1)
        best_incoming = max(best_from_above, best_from_left)
        if best_incoming == IMPOSSIBLE:
            # There is no incoming path.
            return IMPOSSIBLE
        # Extend the best path with the current cell.
        return best_incoming + maze[row][col]
    num_rows = len(maze)
    num_cols = len(maze[0])
    # Return the score of the best path reaching the bottom-right cell.
    return find_best_score_to_cell(num_rows - 1, num_cols - 1)
```

This solution has $O(n^2)$ time complexity and $O(n^2)$ space complexity, since the helper function find_best_score_to_cell may be called at most once per cell.

Solution 2: dynamic programming, bottom-up, $O(n^2)$ time

We can apply the same reasoning but in the opposite order:

- We start from the top-left corner, where we form a path of 1 cell;
- We extend the known paths to the right and below; for any cell, we choose the best path between the one incoming from above and the one incoming from left;
- We set the score to -1 in cells that contain a wall;
- We iterate over cells in an order where the cell above and the cell on the left of the current cell have already had their best score computed.

```
def find_best_path(maze):
    WALL = -1
    IMPOSSIBLE = -1
    num_rows = len(maze)
    num_cols = len(maze[0])
    # best_score_to_cell[row][col] = score of the best path that can reach
    #                                cell (row, col). Initially IMPOSSIBLE.
    best_score_to_cell = [[IMPOSSIBLE] * num_cols for _ in range(num_rows)]
    for row in range(num_rows):
        for col in range(num_cols):
            if maze[row][col] == WALL:
                # No paths can pass through this cell.
                best_score_to_cell[row][col] = IMPOSSIBLE
```

```
            elif row == 0 and col == 0:
                # Starting position: score of the first cell.
                best_score_to_cell[row][col] = maze[row][col]
            else:
                if row > 0:
                    best_from_above = best_score_to_cell[row - 1][col]
                else:
                    # Top row: nothing above.
                    best_from_above = IMPOSSIBLE
                if col > 0:
                    best_from_left = best_score_to_cell[row][col - 1]
                else:
                    # First column: nothing on the left.
                    best_from_left = IMPOSSIBLE
                best_incoming = max(best_from_above, best_from_left)
                if best_incoming == IMPOSSIBLE:
                    # There is no incoming path.
                    best_score_to_cell[row][col] = IMPOSSIBLE
                else:
                    # Extend the best path with the current cell.
                    best_score_to_cell[row][col] = (best_incoming +
                                                    maze[row][col])
    # Return the score of the best path reaching the bottom-right cell.
    return best_score_to_cell[-1][-1]
```

This solution has $O(n^2)$ time complexity and $O(n^2)$ space complexity, since we are iterating over the entire matrix and storing the best score of each cell.

Solution 3: dynamic programming, bottom-up, $O(n^2)$ time, linear space

The iterative solution does not require storing the entire matrix best_score_to_cell, just the last row and the next one to be computed. We can rewrite it in a way that is more memory-efficient:

```
def find_best_path(maze):
    WALL = -1
    IMPOSSIBLE = -1
    num_rows = len(maze)
    num_cols = len(maze[0])
    # best_score_prev_row[col] = score of the best paths that can reach
    #                            the cells on the previous row.
    best_score_prev_row = [IMPOSSIBLE] * num_cols
    # best_score_next_row[col] = score of the best paths that can reach
    #                            the cells on the current row.
    best_score_next_row = [IMPOSSIBLE] * num_cols
    for row in range(num_rows):
```

```
        # Use best_score_prev_row to compute best_score_next_row.
    for col in range(num_cols):
        if maze[row][col] == WALL:
            # No paths can pass through this cell.
            best_score_next_row[col] = IMPOSSIBLE
        elif row == 0 and col == 0:
            # Starting position: score of the first cell.
            best_score_next_row[col] = maze[row][col]
        else:
            if row > 0:
                best_from_above = best_score_prev_row[col]
            else:
                # Top row: nothing above.
                best_from_above = IMPOSSIBLE
            if col > 0:
                best_from_left = best_score_next_row[col - 1]
            else:
                # First column: nothing on the left.
                best_from_left = IMPOSSIBLE
            best_incoming = max(best_from_above, best_from_left)
            if best_incoming == IMPOSSIBLE:
                # There is no incoming path.
                best_score_next_row[col] = IMPOSSIBLE
            else:
                # Extend the best path with the current cell.
                best_score_next_row[col] = (best_incoming +
                                            maze[row][col])
    # Swap buffers.
    best_score_prev_row, best_score_next_row = (best_score_next_row,
                                                best_score_prev_row)
# Return the score of the best path reaching the bottom-right cell.
return best_score_prev_row[-1]
```

This solution has $O(n^2)$ time complexity and $O(n)$ space complexity.

Unit tests

For testing, we first cover simple cases without walls:

```
class TestMaze(unittest.TestCase):
    def test_1_no_walls(self):
        maze = [
            [1, 3],
            [2, 3],
        ]
        self.assertEqual(find_best_path(maze), 7)
```

```
    maze = [
        [1, 2, 1],
        [1, 2, 1],
    ]
    self.assertEqual(find_best_path(maze), 6)
    maze = [
        [1, 1],
        [2, 1],
        [2, 1],
    ]
    self.assertEqual(find_best_path(maze), 6)
```

Then we cover some simple cases with walls:

```
    ...
    def test_2_walls(self):
        maze = [
            [1, -1],
            [1,  1],
        ]
        self.assertEqual(find_best_path(maze), 3)
        maze = [
            [0, -1, 0],
            [0,  1, 0],
        ]
        self.assertEqual(find_best_path(maze), 1)
        maze = [
            [ 0, 0],
            [-1, 1],
            [ 1, 1],
        ]
        self.assertEqual(find_best_path(maze), 2)
        maze = [
            [1, 2, -1],
            [1, 1,  1],
        ]
        self.assertEqual(find_best_path(maze), 5)
```

We also cover some edge cases: a maze with just one cell, and a maze without any paths to the destination:

```
    ...
    def test_3_one_cell_maze(self):
        maze = [
            [2],
        ]
        self.assertEqual(find_best_path(maze), 2)
```

```
    def test_4_no_paths(self):
        maze = [
            [-1],
        ]
        self.assertEqual(find_best_path(maze), -1)
        maze = [
            [ 1, -1],
            [-1,  1],
        ]
        self.assertEqual(find_best_path(maze), -1)
```

Finally, we write a test for large values of n to ensure that the performance is satisfactory:

```
    ...
    def test_5_perf(self):
        n = 50
        maze = [
            [1] * n,
        ] * n
        # All paths pass through 2 * n - 1 cells, each of score 1:
        self.assertEqual(find_best_path(maze), 2 * n - 1)
```

19   Subarray sum

You are given a vector of integers numbers, and a list of queries of the form (start, end). For each query, you must compute the sum of the elements of numbers with indices in [start, end). Return the result as a list.

Example: for numbers = [2, 3, 5, 7, 9], and queries = [(0, 2), (2, 5), (1, 4)], the result is [5, 21, 15] (2 + 3, 5 + 7 + 9, 3 + 5 + 7).

Clarification questions

Q: How large can the array of numbers be?
A: Up to 10,000 numbers.

Q: How many queries can we have?
A: Up to 10,000.

Q: Are the indices in the queries valid?
A: Yes, validation is not necessary.

Solution 1: brute-force, $O(mn)$

The simplest solution is to iterate over the queries, and compute the sum for each query:

```
def subarray_sums(numbers, queries):
    return [sum(numbers[start:end]) for start, end in queries]
```

Assuming that there are up to n numbers and up to m queries, we have m iteration steps, and at each step we perform n - 1 additions. Thus the time complexity is $O(mn)$.

Solution 2: dynamic programming, $O(m + n)$

We notice that the brute-force solution makes a lot of redundant computations when the subarrays from different queries are overlapping:

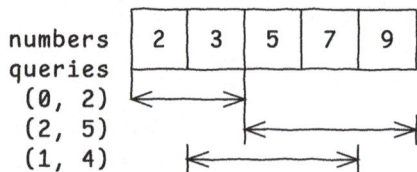

For example, the result of the query (1, 4) can be computed from the result of the previous query (2, 5) by adding 3 and subtracting 9.

This insight is potentially useful, but difficult to use directly, since it is not obvious how to decide efficiently which one of the past queries should be used to compute the current query. The decision would be much easier if we knew that all possible prefixes have been queried:

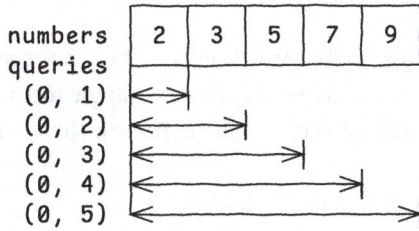

Then any query (`start`, `end`) can be computed from the result of (`0`, `end`) by subtracting the result of (`0`, `start`):

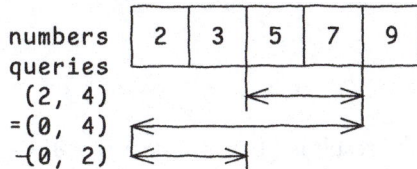

We can compute the prefix sums in advance, incrementally. Then we can compute each query with a single arithmetic operation:

```
def subarray_sums(numbers, queries):
    # prefix_sums[i] = sum of numbers[0:i], 0 <= i <= len(numbers)
    prefix_sums = [0]
    for number in numbers:
        prefix_sums.append(prefix_sums[-1] + number)
    return [prefix_sums[end] - prefix_sums[start]
            for start, end in queries]
```

Computing the prefix sums takes n steps, and solving the queries takes m steps, so the time complexity is $O(m + n)$.

> **Prefix sums**
>
> Prefix sums are very useful: we can use them to compute the sum of a subarray in $O(1)$, among other things. They are used so often that most numerical computing software provides a dedicated function for computing them, usually called cumsum (cumulative sum).

20 Submatrix sum

You are given a matrix of integers, and a list of queries of the form (top, left, bottom, right). For each query, you must compute the sum of the elements of the rectangle formed by matrix cells with row indices in [top, bottom) and [left, right). Return the result as a list.

Example:

```
matrix = [
    [ 1,  2,  3,  4,  5],
    [ 6,  7,  8,  9, 10],
    [11, 12, 13, 14, 15],
    [16, 17, 18, 19, 20],
    [21, 22, 23, 24, 25],
]
```

For queries = [(0, 0, 2, 2), (1, 2, 3, 5)], the result is [1 + 2 + 6 + 7, 8 + 9 + 10 + 13 + 14 + 15].

Clarification questions

Q: How large can the matrix be?
A: Up to 100 rows/columns.

Q: How many queries can we have?
A: Up to 1000.

Q: Are the indices in the queries valid?
A: Yes. Input validation is not necessary.

Hint: this problem is a 2D-version of the subarray sum problem. It is useful to have a good understanding of that before attempting to solve this problem.

Solution 1: brute-force, $O(mn^2)$

The simplest solution is to iterate over the queries, and compute the sum over the rectangle for each query:

```python
def rectangle_sum(matrix, queries):
    result = []
    for top, left, bottom, right in queries:
        rectangle_sum = 0
        for row in matrix[top:bottom]:
            rectangle_sum += sum(row[left:right])
        result.append(rectangle_sum)
    return result
```

Assuming that there are up to n rows and columns and up to m queries, we have m iteration steps, and at each step we perform $O(n^2)$ additions. Thus the time complexity is $O(mn^2)$.

Solution 2: dynamic programming, $O(m + n^2)$

The brute-force solution makes a lot of redundant computations when the rectangles from different queries overlap.

We can compute rectangle sums efficiently if we precompute the sums of all the possible rectangles having top-left corner at (0, 0). Consider an example:

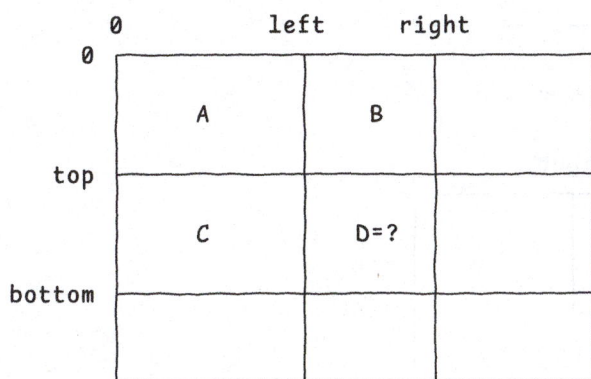

We need to answer the query (top, left, bottom, right). Thus we need to compute D from the figure. If we know the sums of the following rectangles having top-left corner at (0, 0):

- sum(0, 0, bottom, right) = A + B + C + D:

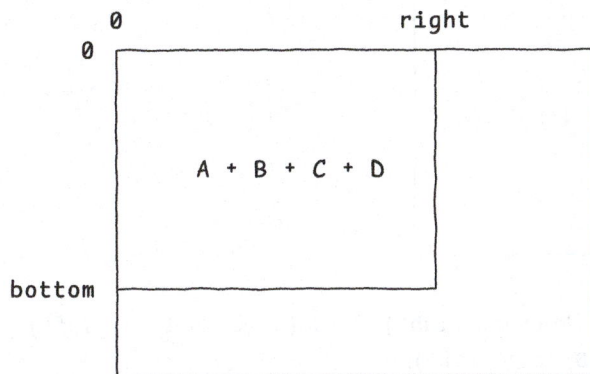

- sum(0, 0, bottom, left) = A + C:

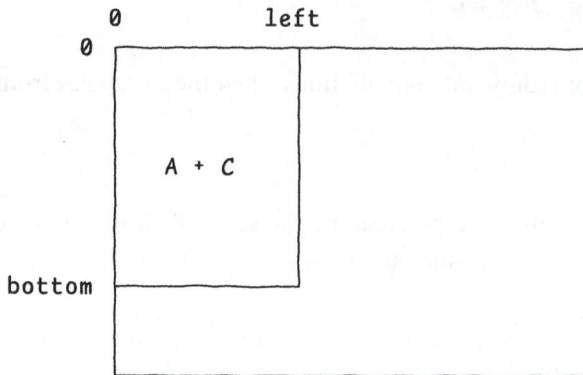

- sum(0, 0, top, right) = A + B:

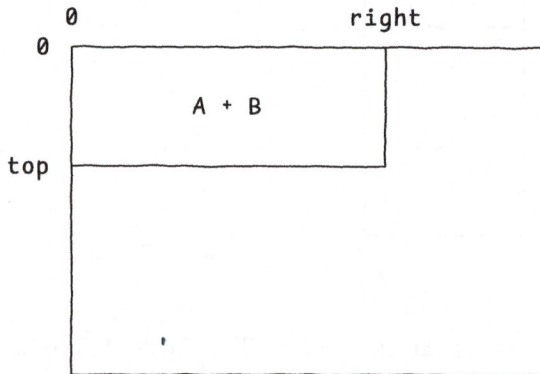

- sum(0, 0, top, left) = A:

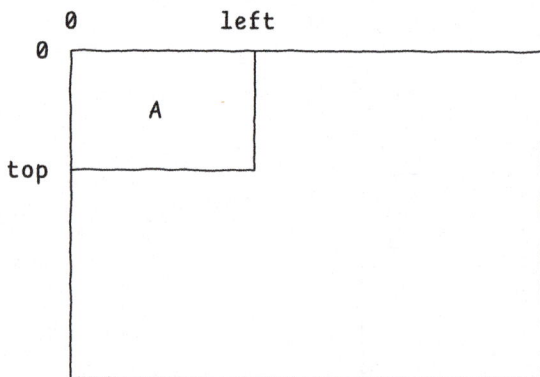

Then we can compute D as sum(0, 0, bottom, right) - sum(0, 0, bottom, left) - sum(0, 0, top, right) + sum(0, 0, top, left).

We store these sums in a matrix prefix_sums which is precomputed. We define prefix_sums[row][col] as the sum of the rectangle from $(0, 0, row, col)$, open-ended, i.e. with indices up to row-1 and col-1, for any 0 <= row <= num_rows and 0 <= col <= num_cols.

Let's take as example a very simple matrix:

`matrix`

1	1	1	1	1
1	1	1	1	1
1	1	1	1	1
1	1	1	1	1
1	1	1	1	1

The procedure to compute `prefix_sums` is the following:

First, we initialize `prefix_sums` with 0. We reserve an extra row and column for queries of the form (0, 0, row, 0) and (0, 0, 0, col):

`prefix_sums`

0	0	0	0	0	0
0	0	0	0	0	0
0	0	0	0	0	0
0	0	0	0	0	0
0	0	0	0	0	0
0	0	0	0	0	0

Then we add the elements of the matrix to the corresponding elements of prefix_sums:

`prefix_sums`

0	0	0	0	0	0
0	1	1	1	1	1
0	1	1	1	1	1
0	1	1	1	1	1
0	1	1	1	1	1
0	1	1	1	1	1

Then we compute running sums in place horizontally:

prefix_sums

0	0	0	0	0	0
0	1	2	3	4	5
0	1	2	3	4	5
0	1	2	3	4	5
0	1	2	3	4	5
0	1	2	3	4	5

Finally, we compute running sums in place vertically:

prefix_sums

	0	1	2	3	4	5
0	0	0	0	0	0	0
1	0	1	2	3	4	5
2	0	2	4	6	8	10
3	0	3	6	9	12	15
4	0	4	8	12	16	20
5	0	5	10	15	20	25

Let's consider a small example to check that it was computed correctly. We answer the query (1, 1, 4, 4), a 3×3 square with sum 9. We compute it as sum(0, 0, 4, 4) - sum(0, 0, 4, 1) - sum(0, 0, 1, 4) + sum(0, 0, 1, 1) = prefix_sums[4][4] - prefix_sums[4][1] - prefix_sums[1][4] + prefix_sums[1][1] = 16 - 4 - 4 + 1 = 9, as expected.

We can implement this algorithm as:

```
def rectangle_sum(matrix, queries):
    num_rows = len(matrix)
    num_cols = len(matrix[0])
    # prefix_sums[row][col] = Sum of the submatrix from (0, 0) to
    #         (row, col), open-ended, i.e. up to row-1 and
    #         col-1 indices.
    #         0 <= row <= num_rows,
    #         0 <= col <= num_cols.
    # Initialize prefix_sums with zeroes.
    prefix_sums = [[0] * (num_cols + 1) for _ in range(num_rows + 1)]
    # Add the elements of the matrix to corresponding elements
    # of prefix_sums.
```

```
for i in range(num_rows):
    for j in range(num_cols):
        prefix_sums[i + 1][j + 1] += matrix[i][j]
# Compute prefix sums horizontally.
for i in range(num_rows):
    for j in range(num_cols):
        prefix_sums[i + 1][j + 1] += prefix_sums[i + 1][j]
# Compute prefix sums vertically.
for i in range(num_rows):
    for j in range(num_cols):
        prefix_sums[i + 1][j + 1] += prefix_sums[i][j + 1]
# Compute the query results.
result = []
for top, left, bottom, right in queries:
    # Ensure top <= bottom and left <= right.
    bottom = max(bottom, top)
    right = max(right, left)
    rectangle_sum = (prefix_sums[bottom][right] -
                     prefix_sums[bottom][left] -
                     prefix_sums[top][right] +
                     prefix_sums[top][left])
    result.append(rectangle_sum)
return result
```

Computing the prefix sums takes $O(n^2)$ steps, and solving the queries takes m steps, so the time complexity is $O(m + n^2)$.

Unit tests

We propose several unit tests.

The first one tests the handling of a very simple example, to ease debugging in case of failure. For this, we use only the value 1 for all matrix elements.

We write a second test that uses distinct matrix elements, to ensure that the code is correct for general cases.

Finally, we write tests that cover edge cases, such as:

- 0×0 submatrix;
- submatrix with height 0;
- submatrix with width 0;
- single-cell submatrix;
- single-column submatrix;
- single-row submatrix;
- submatrix that is a full column of the matrix;
- submatrix that is a full row of the matrix;

- submatrix that equal to the whole matrix;
- empty list of queries.

```python
class TestRectangleSum(unittest.TestCase):
    def test_1_simple(self):
        matrix = [
            [1, 1, 1, 1, 1],
            [1, 1, 1, 1, 1],
            [1, 1, 1, 1, 1],
            [1, 1, 1, 1, 1],
            [1, 1, 1, 1, 1],
        ]
        self.assertEqual(rectangle_sum(matrix,
                                       [
                                           (0, 0, 2, 2),
                                           (1, 1, 4, 4),
                                           (1, 2, 3, 5),
                                       ]),
                                       [
                                           (1 + 1 + 1 + 1),
                                           (1 + 1 + 1 +
                                            1 + 1 + 1 +
                                            1 + 1 + 1),
                                           (1 + 1 + 1 +
                                            1 + 1 + 1)
                                       ])

    def test_2_simple(self):
        matrix = [
            [ 1,  2,  3,  4,  5],
            [ 6,  7,  8,  9, 10],
            [11, 12, 13, 14, 15],
            [16, 17, 18, 19, 20],
            [21, 22, 23, 24, 25],
        ]
        self.assertEqual(rectangle_sum(matrix,
                                       [
                                           (0, 0, 2, 2),
                                           (1, 1, 4, 4),
                                           (1, 2, 3, 5),
                                       ]),
                                       [
                                           (1 + 2 +
                                            6 + 7),
                                           ( 7 + 8 + 9 +
```

```
                                        12 + 13 + 14 +
                                        17 + 18 + 19),
                                      ( 8 +  9 + 10 +
                                        13 + 14 + 15)
                              ])


def test_3_edge_cases(self):
    matrix = [
        [ 1,  2,  3,  4,  5],
        [ 6,  7,  8,  9, 10],
        [11, 12, 13, 14, 15],
        [16, 17, 18, 19, 20],
        [21, 22, 23, 24, 25],
    ]
    # Empty submatrix
    self.assertEqual(rectangle_sum(matrix,
                             [
                                 (1, 1, 1, 1),
                                 (1, 1, 2, 1),
                                 (1, 1, 1, 2),
                                 (1, 1, 0, 0),
                             ]),
                             [
                                 0,
                                 0,
                                 0,
                                 0
                             ])
    # Single-cell, single-column, single-row submatrix
    self.assertEqual(rectangle_sum(matrix,
                             [
                                 (2, 1, 3, 2),
                                 (2, 1, 4, 2),
                                 (2, 1, 3, 3),
                             ]),
                             [
                                 12,
                                 12 + 17,
                                 12 + 13,
                             ])
    # Full-row, full-column, full-matrix submatrix
    self.assertEqual(rectangle_sum(matrix,
                             [
                                 (2, 0, 3, 5),
```

```
                                            (0, 2, 5, 3),
                                            (0, 0, 5, 5),
                                ]),
                                [
                                    11 + 12 + 13 + 14 + 15,
                                    3 + 8 + 13 + 18 + 23,
                                    25 * 26 // 2,
                                ])
        # No queries
        self.assertEqual(rectangle_sum(matrix,
                                    []),
                                    [])
```

21   Largest square submatrix of ones

You are given a matrix where elements are either 0 or 1. Return the number of ones in the largest square-shaped region of the matrix which contains only ones.

Example:

```
matrix = [
    [ 1,  1,  0,  1,  0],
    [ 1,  1,  0,  0,  1],
    [ 0,  1,  1,  1,  0],
    [ 0,  1,  1,  1,  0],
    [ 1,  1,  1,  1,  1],
]
```

The answer is 9 for the 3 × 3 square with top-left corner on the third row and second column.

Clarification questions

Q: How large can the matrix be?
A: Up to 1000 rows/columns.

Q: What answer should be given if the matrix is empty?
A: 0.

Q: Is a single 1 considered a square?
A: Yes.

Solution 1: brute-force, $O(n^5)$

The straightforward solution is to enumerate all the possible squares that contain only ones, computing the area for each one and keeping track of the maximum. We can enumerate all squares by first enumerating all the possible positions of their top-left corner, then iterating over all the possible sizes:

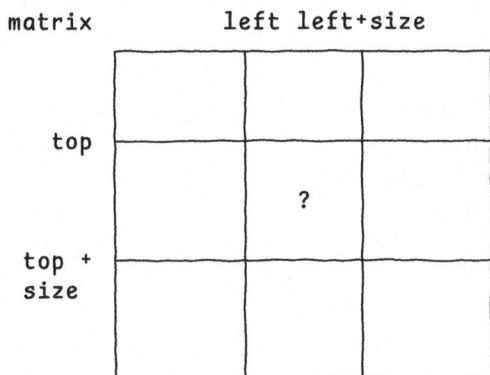

Suppose we write a helper function square_has_only_ones(top, left, size) to check if a square contains only ones. Then the search for the largest square can be written as:

```
def find_largest_square(matrix):
    def square_has_only_ones(top, left, size):
        ...

    num_rows = len(matrix)
    num_cols = len(matrix[0])
    largest = 0
    for top in range(num_rows):
        for left in range(num_cols):
            # Make sure we do not go past the edges of the matrix.
            max_size = min(num_rows - top, num_cols - left)
            for size in range(1, max_size + 1):
                if square_has_only_ones(top, left, size):
                    largest = max(largest, size * size)
    return largest
```

The helper function can be implemented as:

```
def find_largest_square(matrix):
    def square_has_only_ones(top, left, size):
        for row in range(top, top + size):
            for col in range(left, left + size):
                if matrix[row][col] == 0:
                    return False
        return True
    ...
```

We also need to handle the special case of the empty matrix. Putting it all together:

```
def find_largest_square(matrix):
    if not matrix:
        return 0
    num_rows = len(matrix)
    num_cols = len(matrix[0])

    def square_has_only_ones(top, left, size):
        for row in range(top, top + size):
            for col in range(left, left + size):
                if matrix[row][col] == 0:
                    return False
        return True

    largest = 0
    for top in range(num_rows):
        for left in range(num_cols):
            max_size = min(num_rows - top, num_cols - left)
```

```
        for size in range(1, max_size + 1):
            if square_has_only_ones(top, left, size):
                largest = max(largest, size * size)
    return largest
```

The time complexity is $O(n^5)$ due to the 5 nested loops that iterate up to n steps.

Solution 2: dynamic programming, $O(n^2)$

We can reduce complexity by checking if squares are filled with ones in a more efficient way. An idea is to do this incrementally:

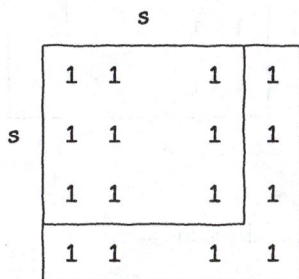

If we already checked that an $s \times s$ square is filled with ones, we can extend it by one row and column. We only have to check if the row and column are filled with ones to determine if the new larger square is also filled with ones. This reduces the complexity of checking that a new square is filled with ones from $O(n^2)$ to $O(n)$.

However we can do better if we look at the structure of the larger square. Any $(s+1) \times (s+1)$ square contains three overlapping $s \times s$ squares:

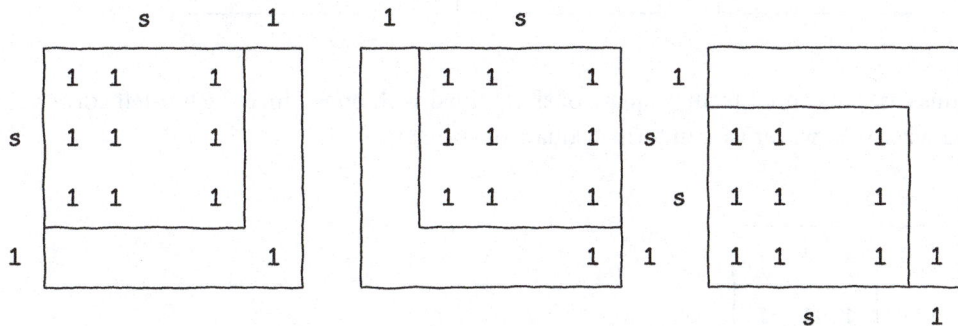

To check if an $(s + 1) \times (s + 1)$ square is filled with ones, it is sufficient to:

- Check if the bottom-right corner contains a one;
- Check if the $s \times s$ square one row above is filled with ones;
- Check if the $s \times s$ square one column to the left is filled with ones;
- Check if the $s \times s$ square one row above and one column to the left is filled with ones.

If the squares on rows above and on columns to the left have already been checked, we can check the $(s + 1) \times (s + 1)$ square incrementally in just $O(1)$ time.

We still have to decide how to handle the cases where some of the checks are failing.

If the the bottom-right corner contains a zero, we cannot form a square filled with ones:

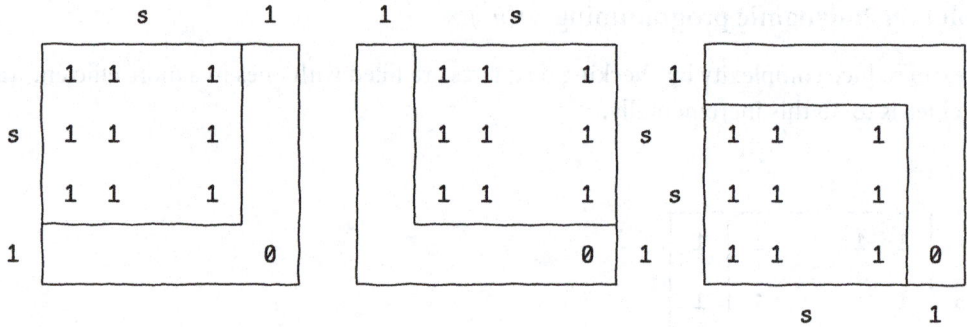

If one or more of the three smaller neighboring squares are not of the same size:

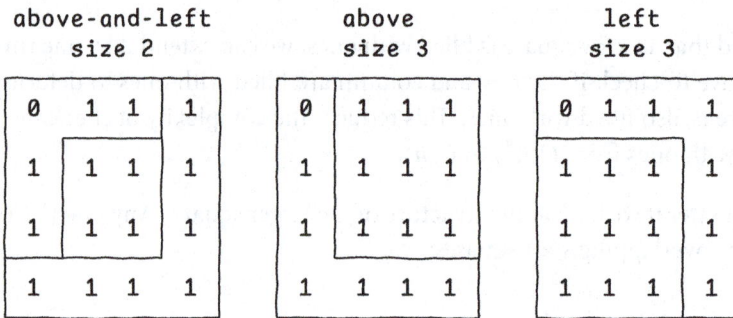

In this case we cannot form a square of size 4 filled with ones, since the top-left corner contains a zero. However we can form a square of size 3:

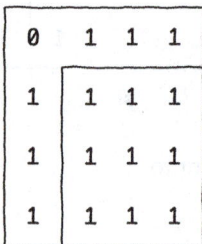

This is equivalent to growing incrementally squares of size 2:

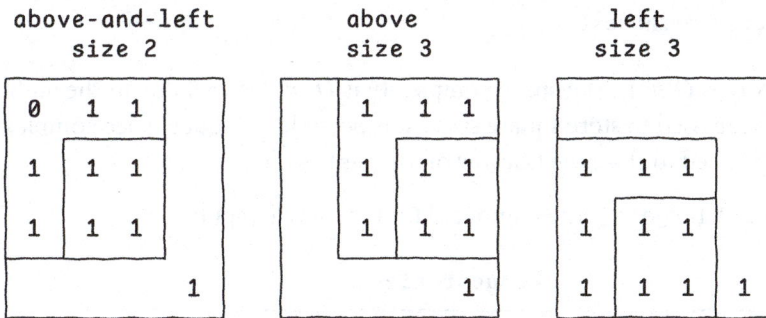

above-and-left size 2 · above size 3 · left size 3

Given the above, let's refine the procedure:

- We iterate over the matrix elements row by row, column by column;
- If the current cell contains a zero, no square filled with ones can be formed there;
- If the current cell contains a one:
    - We read the size s1 of the largest square with bottom-right corner above the cell;
    - We read the size s2 of the largest square with bottom-right corner to the left of the cell;
    - We read the size s3 of the largest square with bottom-right corner above and to the left of the cell;
    - We compute the size of the largest square filled with ones that has bottom-right corner in the cell as min(s1, s2, s3).

We can implement this as:

```python
def find_largest_square(matrix):
    if not matrix:
        return 0
    num_rows = len(matrix)
    num_cols = len(matrix[0])
    # largest_size[row][col] = size of the largest square filled with ones
    #                          having bottom-right corner at (row, col)
    largest_size = [[0] * len(row) for row in matrix]
    largest = 0
    for row in range(num_rows):
        for col in range(num_cols):
            if matrix[row][col] == 0:
                continue
            size_above = largest_size[row - 1][col] if row else 0
            size_left = largest_size[row][col - 1] if col else 0
            size_above_left = (largest_size[row - 1][col - 1]
                               if row and col else 0)
            largest_size[row][col] = 1 + min(size_above,
                                             size_left,
                                             size_above_left)
            largest = max(largest, largest_size[row][col])
```

```
    return largest * largest
```

The time complexity is $O(n^2)$. The space complexity is $O(n^2)$ as well due to the additional matrix largest_size used to store square sizes. It is possible to reduce space complexity to $O(n)$, since we only need to store the last row of largest_size.

Here is an example of largest_size computed for the sample input:

matrix

1	1	0	1	0
1	1	0	0	1
0	1	1	1	0
0	1	1	1	0
1	1	1	1	1

largest_size

1	1	0	1	0
1	2	0	0	1
0	1	1	1	0
0	1	2	2	0
1	1	2	3	1

The largest cell of largest_size has value 3, giving a square size of 9.

22   Largest rectangle in skyline

You are given a skyline where all buildings are rectangular and have the same width. The skyline is encoded as an array of heights.

Return the area of the largest rectangle in the skyline that is covered by buildings.

Example: `skyline = [1, 3, 5, 4, 2, 5, 1]`. The largest rectangle has area 10:

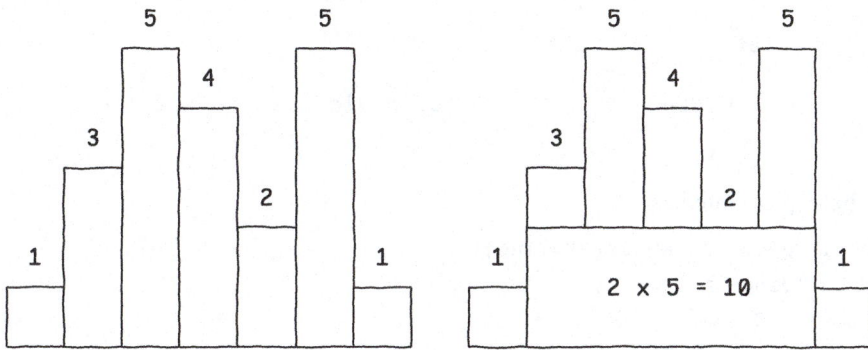

Clarification questions

Q: How large can the array be?
A: Up to 100,000 rows/columns.

Q: What is the largest height?
A: Up to 10,000.

Q: What answer should be given if the array is empty?
A: 0.

Solution 1: brute-force, $O(n^3)$

The simplest solution is to enumerate all possible rectangles, computing the area for each one and keeping track of the maximum. To enumerate all rectangles, we iterate over the left and right edge indices. We then need to compute the minimum height in `heights[left:right+1]` in order to compute the area of the rectangle:

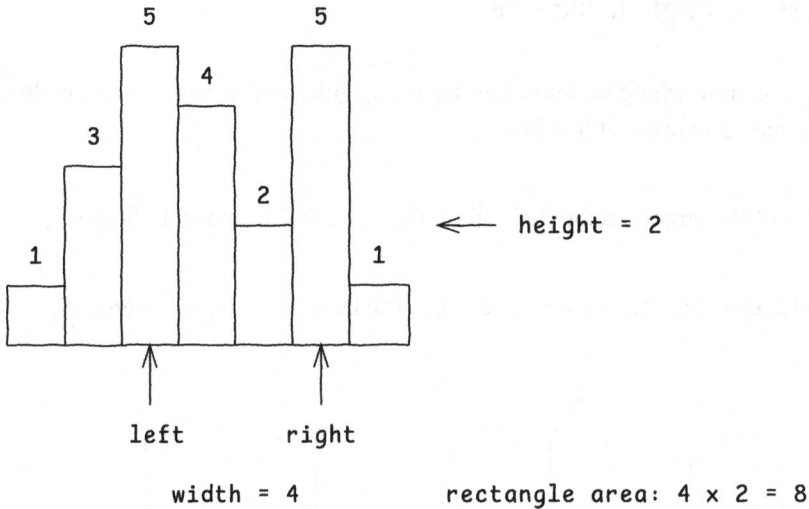

This can be implemented as:

```python
def find_largest_rectangle(skyline):
    num_buildings = len(skyline)
    largest = 0
    for left in range(num_buildings):
        for right in range(left, num_buildings):
            # 0 <= left <= right < len(skyline)
            width = right - left + 1
            height = min(skyline[left:right+1])
            area = width * height
            largest = max(largest, area)
    return largest
```

The time complexity is $O(n^3)$, due to the two nested loops and the time needed to compute the minimum of a subarray at each step.

Solution 2: dynamic programming, $O(n^2)$

We can reduce the time complexity of the previous solution if we reduce the amount of redundant computations we perform. Notice that for each value of `left`, we iterate to the right twice: once to advance the `right` index, and once again to compute `min(skyline[left:right+1])`.

We can reduce this to a single loop by computing the minimum height incrementally: we keep track of the minimum height seen so far in buildings starting from `left`:

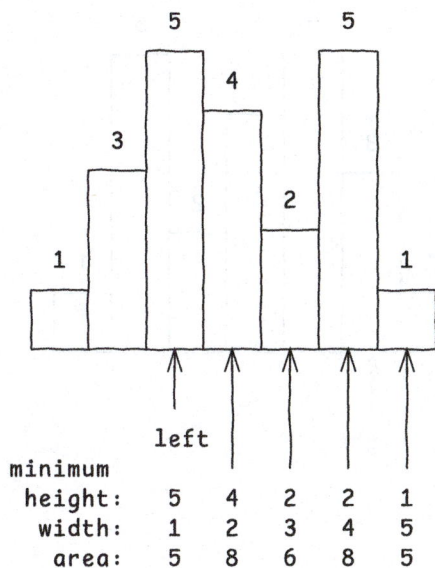

minimum					
height:	5	4	2	2	1
width:	1	2	3	4	5
area:	5	8	6	8	5

This can be written as:

```python
def find_largest_rectangle(skyline):
    num_buildings = len(skyline)
    largest = 0
    for left in range(num_buildings):
        height = skyline[left]
        for right in range(left, num_buildings):
            # 0 <= left <= right < len(skyline)
            width = right - left + 1
            # Compute the new height incrementally:
            height = min(height, skyline[right])
            area = width * height
            largest = max(largest, area)
    return largest
```

The time complexity is $O(n^2)$ due to the two nested loops.

Solution 3: dynamic programming + stack, $O(n)$

We can reduce the complexity further if we notice the following properties of the solution:

- Suppose we move the right pointer through the skyline. Any time the height increases we find a potentially taller rectangle;
- Any time the height decreases, taller buildings from the left cannot contribute to the current rectangle, so their upper parts can be ignored:

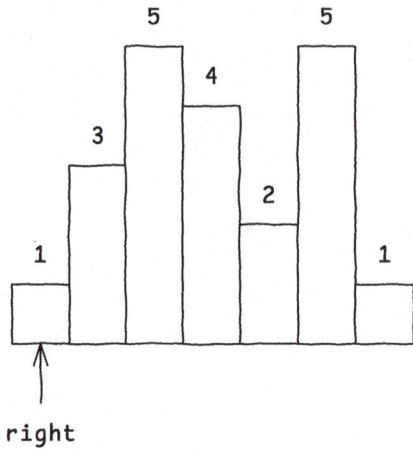

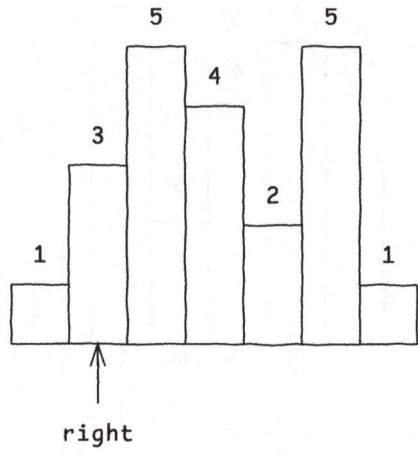

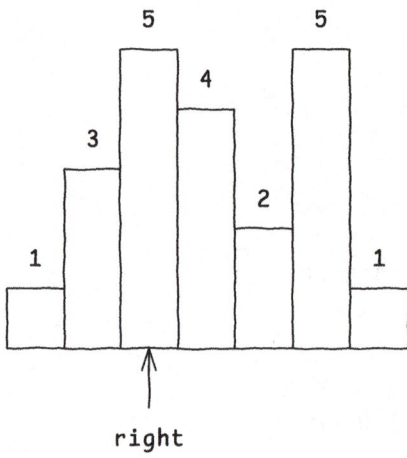

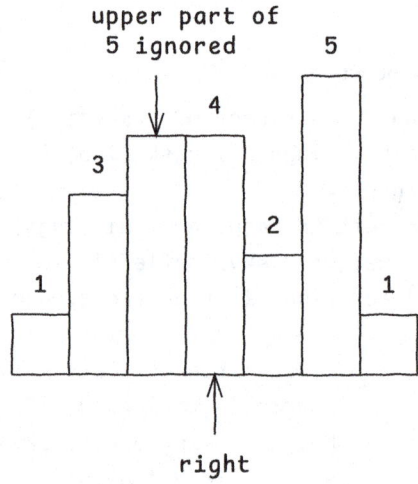

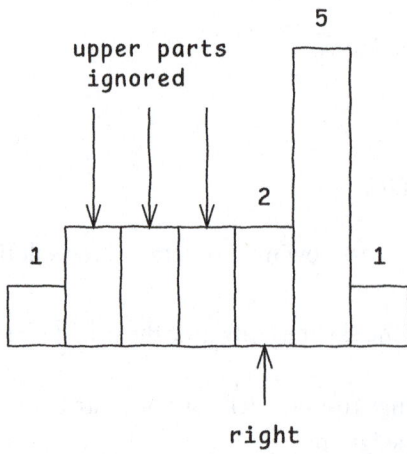

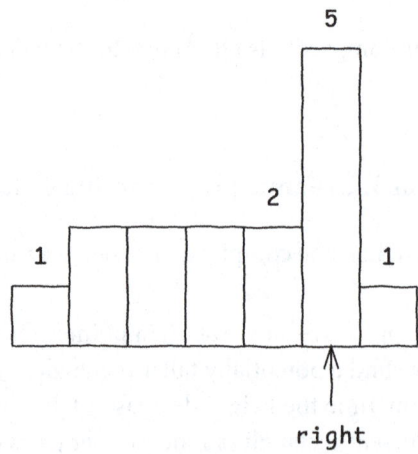

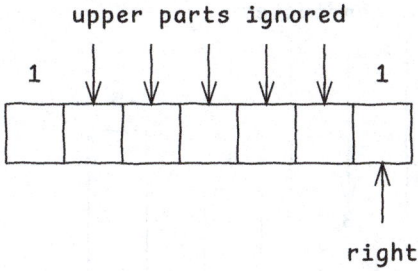

upper parts ignored

Based on this intuition, we can formulate the following solution:

- Iterate with the `right` pointer over the skyline.
- Every time the height increases, grow a list of candidate left pointers.
- When the height decreases, trim the left candidates and update the area on the fly.

Let's see again the iteration as well as how the list of left candidates evolves:

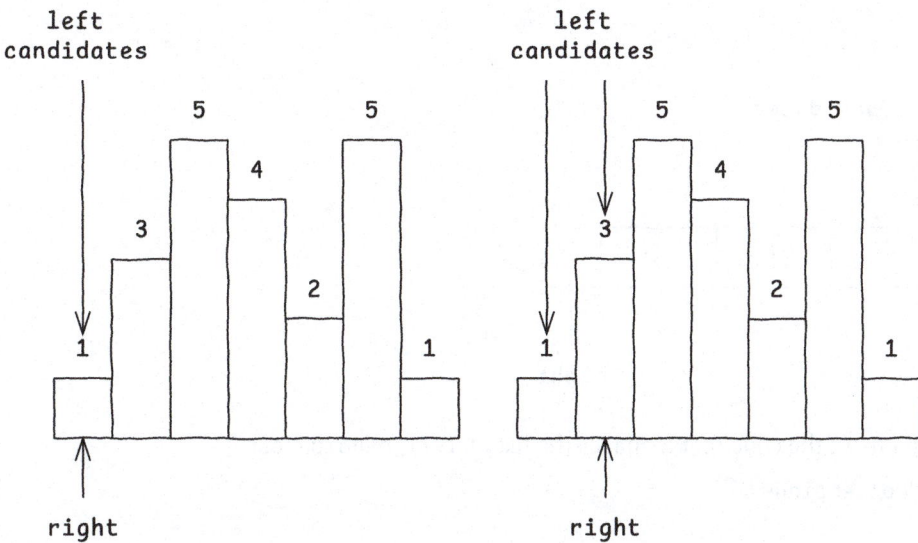

Let's implement the code that manages the list of `left_candidates`:

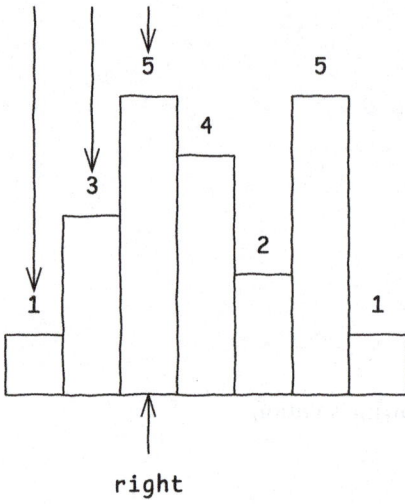

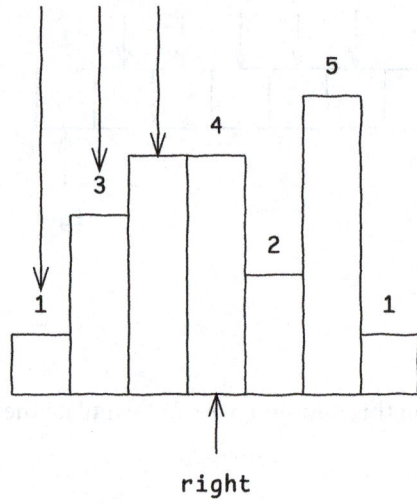

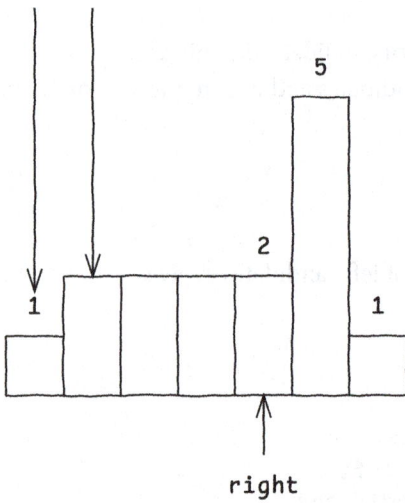

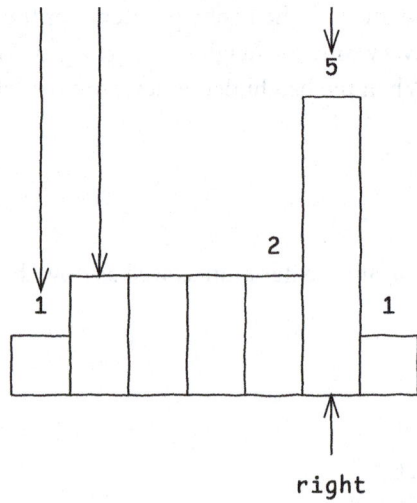

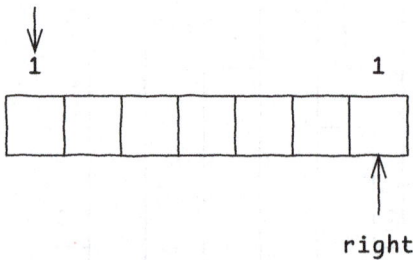

```
import collections
```

```
def find_largest_rectangle(skyline):
    num_buildings = len(skyline)
    Candidate = collections.namedtuple('Candidate', ['index', 'height'])
    left_candidates = []
    for right in range(num_buildings):
        height = skyline[right]
        # Left pointer of the next candidate to be created.
        next_left = right
        while left_candidates and left_candidates[-1].height >= height:
            # TODO update area
            # Possible next candidate by trimming down the building.
            next_left = left_candidates[-1].index
            del left_candidates[-1]
        left_candidates.append(Candidate(index=next_left,
                                         height=height))
    # TODO return result
```

We store each candidate as a named tuple with fields index and height. As we advance the right pointer, we remove left candidates taller than the current building. We keep track of the last trimmed pointer so that we can replace the trimmed buildings with a shorter candidate.

The only thing that we need to do is to update the area. We have two choices: update the area when adding left candidates; or update it when removing left candidates. But when adding left candidates, we cannot do it, since we do not know yet the right pointer. So the only option left is to update it when removing left candidates.

Putting it all together, the code becomes:

```
import collections

def find_largest_rectangle(skyline):
    # Pad the skyline with zero, to avoid having to clean up
    # left_candidates at the end of the iteration.
    skyline = skyline + [0]
    num_buildings = len(skyline)
    Candidate = collections.namedtuple('Candidate', ['index', 'height'])
    left_candidates = []
    largest_area = 0
    for right in range(num_buildings):
        height = skyline[right]
        # Left pointer of the next candidate to be created.
        next_left = right
        while left_candidates and left_candidates[-1].height >= height:
            # Update area.
            # We remove the rectangle starting at left and ending
            # at right-1. It has height left_candidates[-1].height.
```

```
            left = left_candidates[-1].index
            width = right - left
            area = width * left_candidates[-1].height
            largest_area = max(largest_area, area)
            # Possible next candidate by trimming down the building.
            next_left = left
            del left_candidates[-1]
    left_candidates.append(Candidate(index=next_left,
                                     height=height))
    return largest_area
```

Although there are two nested loops, the list of left_candidates is changed with no more than *n* appends/deletes during the entire execution of the algorithm. Thus the time complexity is $O(n)$.

23   Largest submatrix of ones

You are given a matrix where elements are either 0 or 1.

Return the number of ones in the largest rectangular region in the matrix that contains only ones.

Example:

```
matrix = [
    [ 1,  1,  0,  1,  0],
    [ 1,  1,  1,  1,  1],
    [ 0,  1,  1,  1,  1],
    [ 0,  1,  1,  1,  1],
    [ 1,  1,  1,  0,  1],
]
```

The answer is 12 for the 3 × 4 rectangle with top-left corner at (1, 1).

Clarification questions

Q: How large can the matrix be?
A: Up to 1,000 rows/columns.

Q: What answer should be given if the matrix is empty or if it does not contain ones?
A: 0.

Solution 1: brute-force, $O(n^6)$

We first note that a brute-force solution is straightforward:

- Iterate over all possible top-left corners;
  - For each one, iterate over all possible bottom-right corners;
    - Check if the rectangle contains only ones.

This can be implemented as:

```
def find_largest_rectangle(matrix):
    if not matrix:
        return 0
    num_rows = len(matrix)
    num_cols = len(matrix[0])

    def rectangle_has_only_ones(top, left, bottom, right):
        for row in range(top, bottom + 1):
            for col in range(left, right + 1):
                if matrix[row][col] == 0:
                    return False
        return True
```

```
largest = 0
for top in range(num_rows):
    for left in range(num_cols):
        for bottom in range(top, num_rows):
            for right in range(left, num_cols):
                if rectangle_has_only_ones(top, left,
                                                bottom, right):
                    width = right - left + 1
                    height = bottom - top + 1
                    area = width * height
                    largest = max(largest, area)
    return largest
```

Unfortunately the time complexity is a whopping $O(n^6)$, which is too slow.

Solution 2: dynamic programming, $O(n^3)$

We can reduce complexity by checking if rectangles are filled with ones in a more efficient way. An idea is to do this incrementally (similar to the problem of finding the largest square submatrix):

Unfortunately it is more complicated to extend rectangles than squares. For any bottom-right corner, there might be multiple rectangles, any of which could be extended onto the next row/column to form a larger rectangle:

It is too expensive to keep track of all the possible combinations. Therefore, we must find another strategy.

We consider instead smaller rectangles of width 1 (essentially, columns). Any rectangle can be formed by joining together columns of the same height:

Columns can be computed incrementally vertically, row by row:

- Initially columns are formed by ones on the first row;
- When adding the other rows:
    - Each time we see a zero, we clear the column;
    - Each time we see a one, we extend the column.

For example:

0	1	0	1
1	1	1	1
0	1	1	1
1	1	1	1

column sizes

⟵ 1   4   3   4

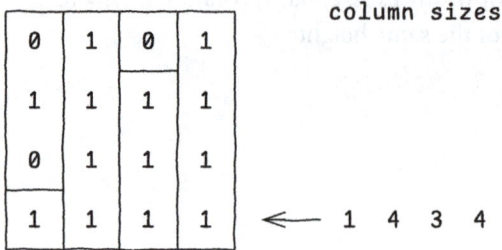

For each step, we try to join together adjacent columns, to form rectangles.

A possible idea is to use a pointer to iterate over columns:

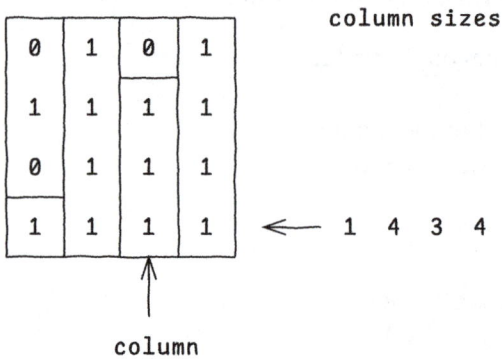

0	1	0	1
1	1	1	1
0	1	1	1
1	1	1	1

column sizes

⟵ 1   4   3   4

column

For the chosen column, we must find how far to the left and to the right we can extend it to form a rectangle. This can be done by comparing the heights of neighboring columns and extending as long as it is greater or equal than the height of the chosen column:

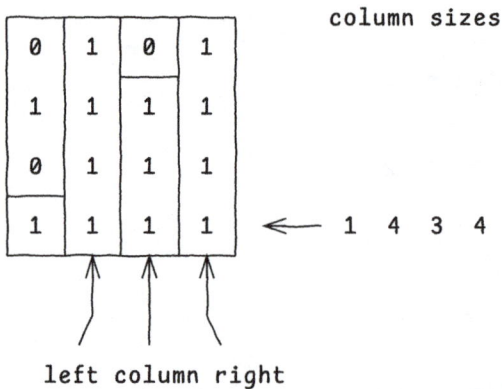

0	1	0	1
1	1	1	1
0	1	1	1
1	1	1	1

column sizes

⟵ 1   4   3   4

left column right

This algorithm can be implemented as:

```python
def find_largest_rectangle(matrix):
    if not matrix:
        return 0
    num_rows = len(matrix)
    num_cols = len(matrix[0])
```

```
# column_heights[i] = height of i-th column
column_heights = [0] * num_cols
largest = 0
for row in range(num_rows):
    # Update column_heights
    for col in range(num_cols):
        if matrix[row][col] == 0:
            # Reset column
            column_heights[col] = 0
        else:
            # Extend column
            column_heights[col] += 1
    # Find largest rectangle with lower edge on the row
    for col in range(num_cols):
        height = column_heights[col]
        # Find leftmost edge:
        left = col
        while (left - 1 >= 0 and
                column_heights[left-1] >= height):
            left -= 1
        # Find rightmost edge:
        right = col
        while (right + 1 < num_cols
                and column_heights[right+1] >= height):
            right += 1
        # Compute rectangle's area
        width = right - left + 1
        area = width * height
        # Update maximum overall
        largest = max(largest, area)
return largest
```

The time complexity is $O(n^3)$ due to the three nested loops.

Solution 3: dynamic programming, $O(n^2)$

Notice that the step of finding the largest rectangle once we computed the column sizes is the same as the problem of finding the largest rectangle inside a skyline.

For example, the following are equivalent:

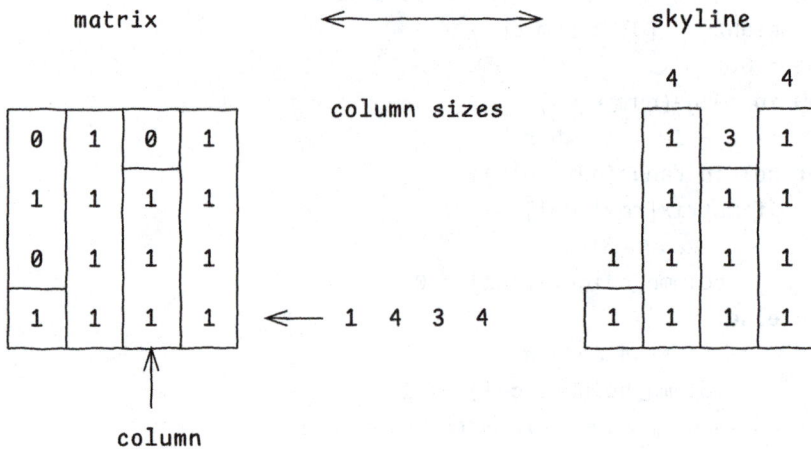

We can thus use the $O(n)$ solution of the problem at each step, for an overall complexity of $O(n^2)$:

```python
def find_largest_rectangle(matrix):
    if not matrix:
        return 0
    num_rows = len(matrix)
    num_cols = len(matrix[0])
    # column_heights[i] = height of i-th column
    column_heights = [0] * num_cols
    largest = 0
    for row in range(num_rows):
        # Update column_heights
        for col in range(num_cols):
            if matrix[row][col] == 0:
                # Reset column
                column_heights[col] = 0
            else:
                # Extend column
                column_heights[col] += 1
        # Find largest rectangle with lower edge on the row
        area = find_largest_rectangle_skyline(column_heights)
        # Update maximum overall
        largest = max(largest, area)
    return largest
```

We will not repeat the code that implements find_largest_rectangle_skyline since it has been already solved and explained in the previous problem.

24 Interleaved strings

You are given two input strings and an output string. Check if the output string can be obtained by interleaving all the characters of the two input strings, maintaining the order in which they appear in the input strings.

Example 1: Given input strings "abc" and "def", and output string "adbcef", the output string can be obtained by interleaving in the following way:

- take character 'a' from the first string;
- take character 'd' from the second string;
- take characters 'b' and 'c' from the first string;
- take characters 'e' and 'f' from the second string.

Example 2: Given input strings "abc" and "def", and output string "deabfc", the output string can be obtained by interleaving in the following way:

- take characters 'd' and 'e' from the second string;
- take characters 'a' and 'b' from the first string;
- take character 'f' from the second string;
- take character 'c' from the first string.

Example 3: Given input strings "abc" and "def", and output string "bacdef", the output string cannot be obtained by interleaving. This is because characters 'b' and 'a' appear in the wrong order in the output string.

Example 4: Given input strings "abc" and "def", and output string "aabcdef", the output string cannot be obtained by interleaving. This is because there is an extra occurrence of 'a' in the output string.

Clarification questions

Q: How large can the strings be?
A: Up to 1,000 characters each.

Q: What answer should be given if all strings are empty?
A: True.

Solution 1: brute-force, $O(2^n)$

When the first characters of the input strings are distinct, it is straightforward to compute the interleaving. There are several cases:

- The output string starts with the first character of the first input string:

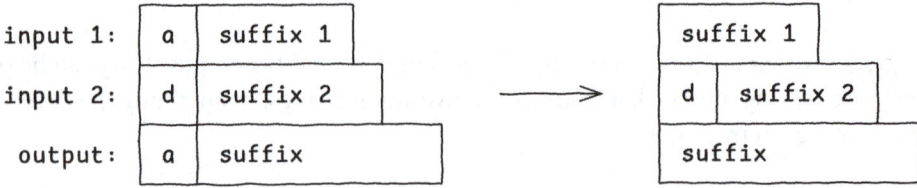

In this case we can consume the first character of the first input string and the first character of the output string, then continue the interleaving with the rest of the characters.

- The output string starts with the first character of the second input string:

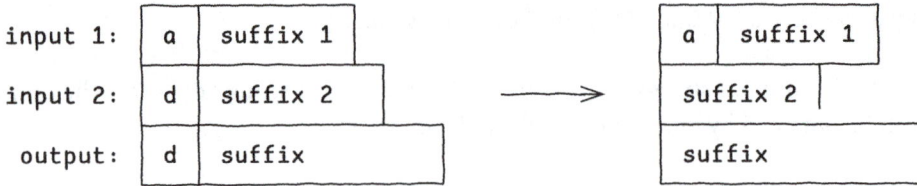

In this case we can consume the first character of the second input string and the first character of the output string, then continue the interleaving with the rest of the characters.

- The output string does not start with the first character of either input string:

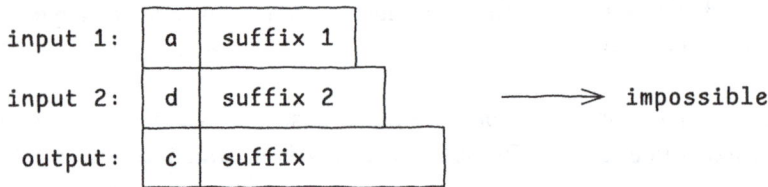

In this case we cannot form the output string by interleaving the input strings, so we can return the answer False.

- The first input string is empty:

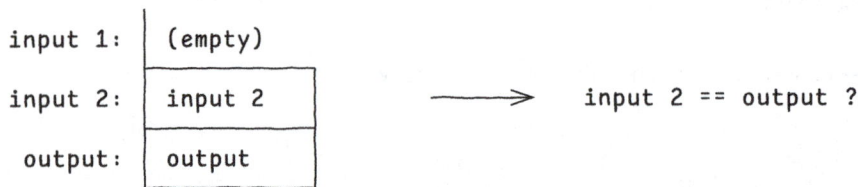

We consumed the first input string.

We have to check if the second input is equal to the output, since that is the only way to perform the rest of the interleaving.

- The second input string is empty:

```
input 1:  | input 1  |
input 2:  | (empty)  |          ———————>      input 1 == output ?
output:   | output   |
```

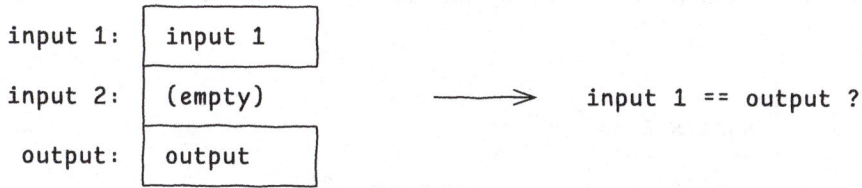

We consumed the second input string.

We have to check if the first input string is equal to the output string, since that is the only way to perform the rest of the interleaving.

- Both input strings are empty:

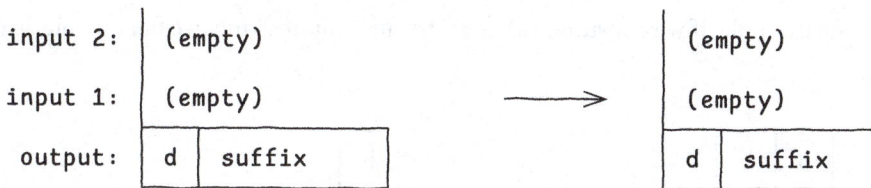

```
input 2:  | (empty)       |                  | (empty)       |
input 1:  | (empty)       |       ——————>    | (empty)       |
output:   | d | suffix    |                  | d | suffix    |
```

We consumed all characters from the input strings, but we still have to emit characters in the output string. This makes the interleaving impossible.

- The output string is empty:

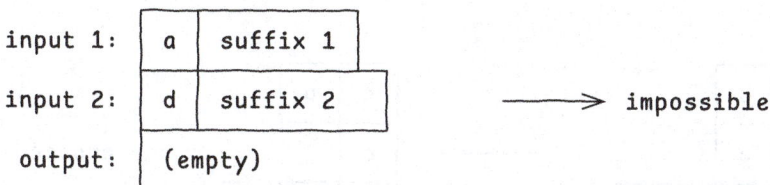

```
input 1:  | a | suffix 1  |
input 2:  | d | suffix 2  |       ——————>    impossible
output:   | (empty)       |
```

In this case the output string has more characters than the input strings taken together, so we cannot obtain it by interleaving.

- All strings are empty:

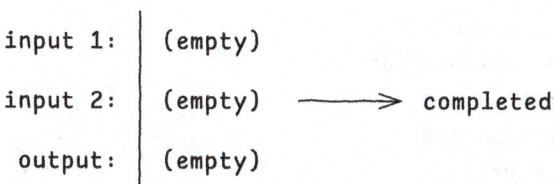

```
input 1:  | (empty)
input 2:  | (empty)    ——————>  completed
output:   | (empty)
```

We consumed all characters from all three strings, in which case we return true, since the interleaving has been completed.

Unfortunately, there is one more case left in which the way to continue the interleaving is ambiguous:

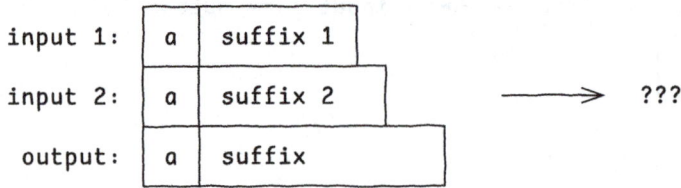

| input 1: | a | suffix 1 |
| input 2: | a | suffix 2 | ⟶ ???
| output: | a | suffix |

When the first character of both input strings are equal and match the first character of the output string, we do not know whether we should consume a character from the first input string or from the second one. Both choices are equally valid, but it is possible that only one of them may lead to a successful interleaving.

In the following example, if we consume 'a' from the first input string, we fail the interleaving:

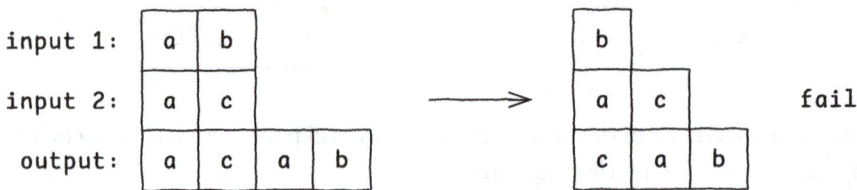

| input 1: | a | b |
| input 2: | a | c | ⟶
| output: | a | c | a | b |

| | b |
| a | c | fail
| c | a | b |

However, if we consume it instead from the second input string, we can complete the interleaving:

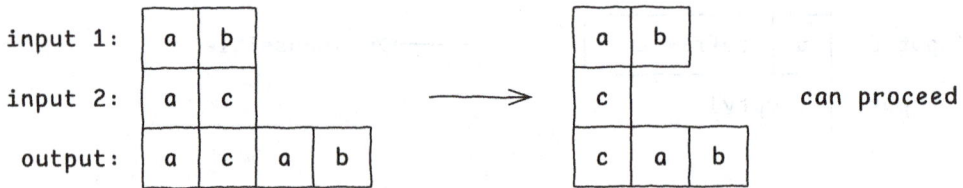

| input 1: | a | b |
| input 2: | a | c | ⟶
| output: | a | c | a | b |

| a | b |
| c |
| c | a | b | can proceed

Therefore, when the first character is the same in all three strings, we have no choice but to try both options.

This logic can be implemented as:

```python
def can_interleave(input1, input2, output):
    def check(index_in1, index_in2, index_out):
        if (index_in1 == len(input1) and
            index_in2 == len(input2) and
            index_out == len(output)):
            # We matched everything: interleaving completed.
            return True
        # We use string[i:i+1] to handle in one-shot also empty strings.
```

```
        # If string is empty, then string[i:i+1] is also empty.
        first_in1 = input1[index_in1:index_in1+1]
        first_in2 = input2[index_in2:index_in2+1]
        first_out = output[index_out:index_out+1]
        if first_in1 == first_in2 == first_out:
            # We do not know which way to continue, try both options:
            return (check(index_in1 + 1, index_in2, index_out + 1) or
                    check(index_in1, index_in2 + 1, index_out + 1))
        if first_in1 == first_out:
            # Consume the first character of input 1.
            return check(index_in1 + 1, index_in2, index_out + 1)
        elif first_in2 == first_out:
            # Consume the first character of input 2.
            return check(index_in1, index_in2 + 1, index_out + 1)
        else:
            # First character mismatches in both inputs.
            return False
    return check(0, 0, 0)
```

The time complexity is $O(2^n)$ due to the ambiguous check. For inputs where there are no ambiguous characters, the running time is $O(n)$.

Solution 2: dynamic programming, $O(n^2)$

The function check(index_in1, index_in2, index_out) takes three parameters, which are the current indices in the three strings.

The index in the output string is always the sum of the indices in the two input strings (due to the logic we use at each step to consume a character from exactly one of the inputs as well as consuming a character from the output).

Therefore, we can simplify the function call as check(index_in1, index_in2).

The check function takes as parameters the two indices, which can take values from well defined intervals: 0 <= index_in1 <= len(input1), 0 <= index_in2 <= len(input2). So overall there can be only len(input1) * len(input2) different combinations of possible arguments in its calls.

Yet in the previous section we have seen that the time complexity of the algorithm is $O(2^n)$, due to an exponential number of calls of the check function. Since the number of possible arguments is only $O(n^2)$, this means that many of the calls are redundant.

In addition, the check function does not have any side effects: it does not change the contents of the strings. So it returns the same result when called repeatedly with the same arguments.

Therefore, we can simply cache the result of the function to achieve $O(n^2)$ complexity:

```python
def can_interleave(input1, input2, output):
    @lru_cache(maxsize=None)
    def check(index_in1, index_in2):
        index_out = index_in1 + index_in2
        if (index_in1 == len(input1) and
            index_in2 == len(input2) and
            index_out == len(output)):
            # We matched everything: interleaving completed.
            return True
        # We use string[i:i+1] to handle in one-shot also empty strings.
        # If string is empty, then string[i:i+1] is also empty.
        first_in1 = input1[index_in1:index_in1+1]
        first_in2 = input2[index_in2:index_in2+1]
        first_out = output[index_out:index_out+1]
        if first_in1 == first_in2 == first_out:
            # We do not know which way to continue, try both options:
            return (check(index_in1 + 1, index_in2) or
                    check(index_in1, index_in2 + 1))
        if first_in1 == first_out:
            # Consume the first character of input 1.
            return check(index_in1 + 1, index_in2)
        elif first_in2 == first_out:
            # Consume the first character of input 2.
            return check(index_in1, index_in2 + 1)
        else:
            # First character mismatches in both inputs.
            return False
    return check(0, 0)
```

25 Regular expression matching

Check if a string matches a regular expression. The regular expression language must implement the '.' and '*' operators:

- '.' matches any character;
- '*' causes the matching rule before it to be applied any number of times (including zero).

Examples:

- "abc" matches the regular expression "abc";
- "abc" matches the regular expression "a.c";
- "abbc" matches the regular expression "ab*c";
- "ac" matches the regular expression "ab*c";
- "ac" matches the regular expression "a.*c";
- "abcd" matches the regular expression "a.*d".

Clarification questions

Q: How large can the inputs be?
A: Both the input string and the regular expression can have up to 100 characters.

Q: How should we handle invalid regular expressions? For example, '*' or 'a**'.
A: You may choose to handle errors if you wish, but it is optional.

Solution 1: brute-force, $O(2^n)$

Let's look at how regular expression rules work with a few examples:

- When the regular expression starts with a character that is not followed by '*', we must consume a character from the input if possible, while at the same time consuming the character from the regular expression:

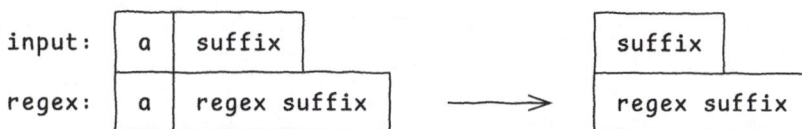

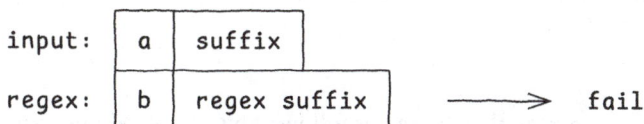

input:	a	suffix		suffix	
regex:	a	regex suffix	$\longrightarrow$	regex suffix	

input:	a	suffix			
regex:	b	regex suffix	$\longrightarrow$	fail	

- When the regular expression starts with a '.' that is not followed by '*', we must consume a character from the input if possible, while at the same time consuming the '.' from the regular expression:

```
input:   | a | suffix       |              | suffix       |
regex:   | . | regex suffix |    ─────>    | regex suffix |

input:   | (empty)         |
regex:   | . | regex suffix |   ─────>    fail
```

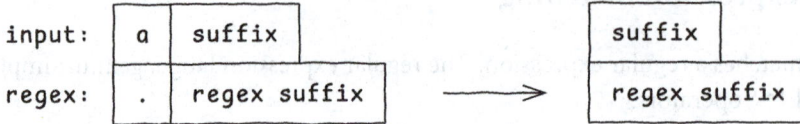

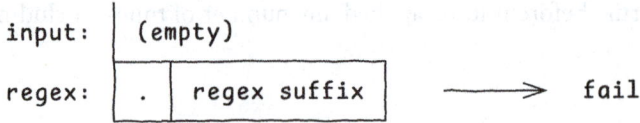

- When the input string and the regular expression are both empty, we have a match:

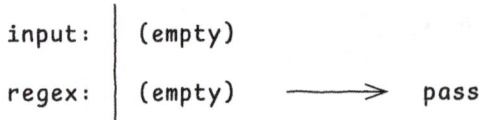

```
input:   | (empty)
regex:   | (empty)     ─────>    pass
```

- When the regular expression is empty and the input string is not empty, we fail the match:

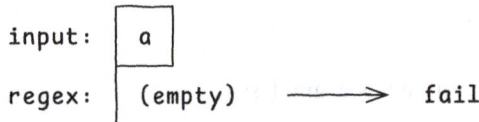

```
input:   | a |
regex:   | (empty)    ─────>    fail
```

- When the input string is empty and the regular expression starts with a character, we fail the match:

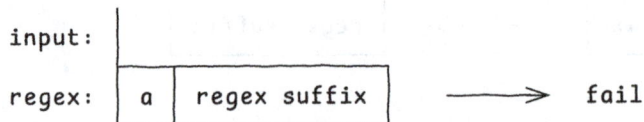

```
input:   |
regex:   | a | regex suffix |   ─────>    fail
```

- When the regular expression starts with a character followed by '*', we do not know how many occurrences of that character we should consume. So we have no choice but to try all possible options. We can reduce these to either consuming the regex prefix without consuming a character, or consuming a character (if it is matching) without consuming the regex prefix:

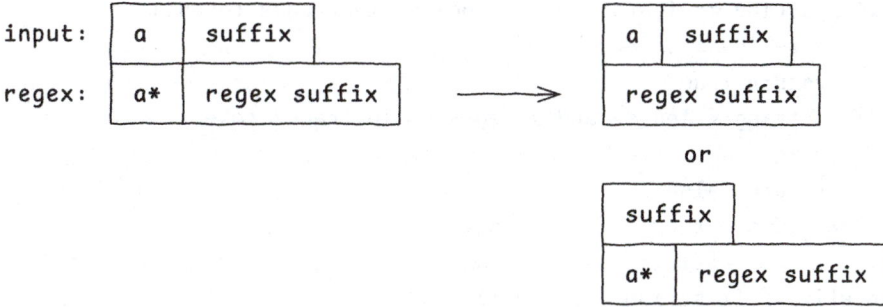

However when the input does not match, there is a single option, consuming the regular expression prefix:

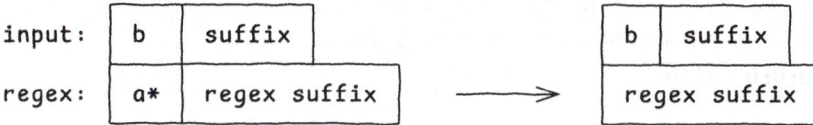

- When the regular expression starts with '.*', we have two options: consume the regular expression prefix without consuming anything from the string, or consume the first character of the string without consuming the regular expression prefix:

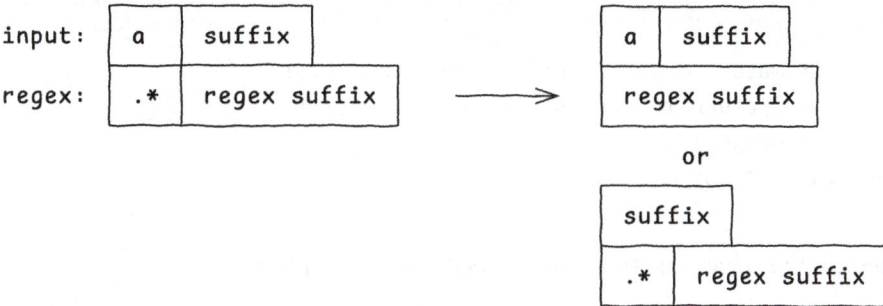

These rules can be implemented recursively with a helper function match that takes as parameters the offset in the input string and the offset in the regular expression:

```python
def regex_match(s, regex):
    # TODO: implement helper parse_regex() to split regex into atomic parts
    # TODO: implement helper match_no_star() to check simple prefix match
    regex_tokens = parse_regex()

    def match(i_string, i_regex):
        """
        Checks if it is possible to match s[i_string:] with
        regex_tokens[i_regex:].
        """
```

```python
        if i_string == len(s) and i_regex == len(regex_tokens):
            # We found a match.
            return True
        if i_string < len(s) and i_regex == len(regex_tokens):
            # We cannot consume any more string characters.
            return False
        # prefix = either the i_string-th character or
        #          the empty string (when we reach the end of the string).
        prefix = s[i_string:i_string+1]
        regex_token = regex_tokens[i_regex]
        if regex_token[-1] != '*':
            # Handle a token like 'a' or '.'.
            # Consume 1 chars and the regex token.
            if match_no_star(prefix, regex_token):
                return match(i_string + 1, i_regex + 1)
            return False
        else:
            # Handle a token like 'a*' or '.*'.
            # Try to consume 0 chars and the regex token.
            if match(i_string, i_regex + 1):
                return True
            # Try to consume 1 char, do not consume the regex token.
            # This is because we might want to use the token again to
            # consume more chars.
            if match_no_star(prefix, regex_token[0]):
                return match(i_string + 1, i_regex)
            return False
    return match(0, 0)
```

Let's implement the helper function that parses the regular expression:

```python
def parse_regex():
    """
    Parse the regex into a list of tokens, each like one of:
    - 'a'
    - '.'
    - 'a*'
    - '.*'
    """

    tokens = []
    for c in regex:
        if c == '*':
            if not tokens or tokens[-1][-1] == '*':
                raise ValueError('* must be preceded by character')
            tokens[-1] += '*'
```

```
        else:
            tokens.append(c)
    return tokens
```

And here is the helper function that checks a simple prefix match:

```
def match_no_star(c, regex_token):
    """
    Match a character to a regex_token that does not contain '*'.
    Handles also c == ''.
    """
    assert len(regex_token) == 1
    if regex_token == '.':
        # Any character matches '.'. The empty string does not.
        return len(c) == 1
    # Match a character with another.
    return c == regex_token
```

Let's perform the complexity analysis of the match function. For regular expressions without stars, the function advances in tandem the indices in the input string and the regular expression, so the running time is $O(n)$, where n = max(len(s), len(regex)).

However, for regular expressions containing the star operator, it may make up to 2 calls at each step, which causes the time complexity to reach $O(2^n)$.

Solution 2: dynamic programming, $O(n^2)$

The match(i_string, i_regex) function takes as arguments the two indices, which can take values from well defined intervals: 0 <= i_string <= len(s), 0 <= i_regex <= len(regex_tokens). Overall, there can be only len(s) * len(regex_tokens), thus $O(n^2)$, different combinations of possible inputs.

Yet in the previous section we have seen that the time complexity of the algorithm is $O(2^n)$, due to a potentially exponential number of calls of the check function on certain inputs. Since the number of possible arguments is only $O(n^2)$, many of the calls are redundant.

For example, for the input string "aaaxyz" and regular expression "a*a*a*a*a*xyq", there are a lot of different ways to reach the call that checks the match between "xyz" and "xyq".

We must eliminate the redundant calls to reduce the time complexity. This can be achieved simply by caching the results. In this way, we guarantee that no more than $O(n^2)$ calls of the function are executed, reducing time complexity to $O(n^2)$:

```
from functools import lru_cache


def regex_match(s, regex):
    def parse_regex():
        """
```

```
    Parse the regex into a list of tokens, each like one of:
    - 'a'
    - '.'
    - 'a*'
    - '.*'
    """

    tokens = []
    for c in regex:
        if c == '*':
            if not tokens or tokens[-1][-1] == '*':
                raise ValueError('* must be preceded by character')
            tokens[-1] += '*'
        else:
            tokens.append(c)
    return tokens


def match_no_star(c, regex_token):
    """
    Match a character to a regex_token that does not contain '*'.
    Handles also c == ''.
    """

    assert len(regex_token) == 1
    if regex_token == '.':
        # Any character matches '.'. The empty string does not.
        return len(c) == 1
    # Match a character with another.
    return c == regex_token


regex_tokens = parse_regex()
@lru_cache(maxsize=10000)
def match(i_string, i_regex):
    """
    Checks if it is possible to match s[i_string:] to tokens[i_regex:].
    """

    if (i_string == len(s) and
        i_regex == len(regex_tokens)):
        # We found a match.
        return True
    if i_regex == len(regex_tokens):
        # We cannot consume any more string characters.
        return False
    # Prefix is either the i_string-th character or
    # the empty string when we reach the end of the string.
    prefix = s[i_string:i_string+1]
```

```
        token = regex_tokens[i_regex]
        if token[-1] != '*':
            # Handle a token like 'a' or '.'.
            # Consume 1 chars and the regex token.
            if match_no_star(prefix, token):
                return match(i_string + 1, i_regex + 1)
            return False
        else:
            # Handle a token like 'a*' or '.*'.
            # Try to consume 0 chars and the regex token.
            if match(i_string, i_regex + 1):
                return True
            # Try to consume 1 char, do not consume the regex token.
            # This is because we might want to use the token again to
            # consume more chars.
            elif match_no_star(prefix, token[0]):
                return match(i_string + 1, i_regex)
            return False
    return match(0, 0)
```

Unit tests

We propose the following unit tests:

- Simple tests that check matching with regular expressions containing only regular characters and wildcards (no stars);
- Tests that check matching with regular expressions containing a character star;
- Tests that check matching with regular expressions containing a '.*';
- Tests that check matching with regular expressions containing multiple stars;
- A performance test that uses large, problematic inputs.

```
class TestRegexMatching(unittest.TestCase):
    def test_1_simple(self):
        self.assertTrue(regex_match('abc', 'abc'))
        self.assertTrue(regex_match('abc', 'a.c'))
        self.assertTrue(regex_match('abc', '...'))
        self.assertFalse(regex_match('abx', 'abc'))
        self.assertFalse(regex_match('abx', 'a.c'))
        self.assertFalse(regex_match('ab', '...'))
        self.assertTrue(regex_match('', ''))

    def test_2_star(self):
        self.assertTrue(regex_match('', 'b*'))
        self.assertTrue(regex_match('b', 'b*'))
        self.assertTrue(regex_match('bb', 'b*'))
        self.assertTrue(regex_match('ac', 'ab*c'))
```

```python
        self.assertTrue(regex_match('abc', 'ab*c'))
        self.assertTrue(regex_match('abbc', 'ab*c'))
        self.assertFalse(regex_match('axc', 'ab*c'))
        self.assertFalse(regex_match('a', 'b*'))
        self.assertFalse(regex_match('ba', 'b*'))

    def test_3_star_dot(self):
        self.assertTrue(regex_match('ac', 'a.*c'))
        self.assertTrue(regex_match('abc', 'a.*c'))
        self.assertTrue(regex_match('abbc', 'a.*c'))
        self.assertTrue(regex_match('abxc', 'a.*c'))
        self.assertTrue(regex_match('abcc', 'a.*c'))
        self.assertFalse(regex_match('ax', 'a.*c'))

    def test_4_multiple_stars(self):
        self.assertTrue(regex_match('', 'a*b*c*'))
        self.assertTrue(regex_match('a', 'a*b*c*'))
        self.assertTrue(regex_match('ab', 'a*b*c*'))
        self.assertTrue(regex_match('abc', 'a*b*c*'))
        self.assertTrue(regex_match('xabcy', 'xa*b*c*y'))
        self.assertTrue(regex_match('zabcy', '.a*b*c*y'))
        self.assertTrue(regex_match('xabcy', 'x.*.*y'))
        self.assertTrue(regex_match('', 'x*.*.*.*y*'))
        self.assertFalse(regex_match('xabcz', 'x.*.*y'))

    def test_5_perf(self):
        n = 100
        self.assertTrue(regex_match('a' * n, 'a*' * n))
        self.assertTrue(regex_match('a' * n, '.*' * n))
        self.assertFalse(regex_match('a' * n + 'x', 'a*' * n + 'y'))
        self.assertFalse(regex_match('a' * n + 'x', '.*' * n + 'y'))
```

Made in the USA
Monee, IL
08 January 2025

76352634R00103